UNDERSTANDING VIDEO EQUIPMENT

UNDERSTANDING VIDEO EQUIPMENT

Design, Operation and Maintenance of Videotape Recorders and Cameras

Neil Heller

Knowledge Industry Publications, Inc.,
White Plains, NY

The Video Bookshelf

UNDERSTANDING VIDEO EQUIPMENT:
Design and Maintenance of Videotape Recorders and Cameras

Neil Heller

ISBN 0-86729-184-2 (hardcover)
ISBN 0-86729-185-0 (student edition)

Printed in the United States of America

Copyright © 1989 by Knowledge Industry Publications, Inc., 701 Westchester Ave.,
White Plains, NY 10604.

10 9 8 7 6 5 4 3 2 1

Table of Contents

Tables and Figures

Foreword

An old saying talks about the success of any venture in terms of finding a need and filling it. When it came to the need for writing this book, the need found me. For many years, while teaching seminars on the technical and application aspects of video equipment, I was asked by students where they could find a reference book on video equipment. Although many technical books have been written on video equipment, none combined both the technical and applications approaches. The challenge was to write a book that could be used to solve a variety of daily problems encountered by both technical and nontechnical readers.

For video managers this book can be used as an aid to understanding the inner workings of cameras and videotape recorders. For the more technically inclined, the book offers a theoretical approach to the basics of troubleshooting and repairing video equipment that can be universally applied regardless of manufacturer. For both there are chapters covering the interpretation of waveforms as they appear on waveform monitors and vectorscopes.

The book has been divided into two parts: Part 1 covers videotape recorders while Part 2 focuses on video cameras. Each of these devices is fundamental to the operation of the video system—one is used for creating the video picture, the other for recording it. Both work together to create a video production. However, determining needs and understanding specifications and operations are simpler to understand if they are treated separately.

It is my hope that this book will serve as a reference to the thousands of workshop attendees I have had the privilege of coming in contact with.

A project of this size could never have been possible without the help of numerous individuals and manufacturers. To attempt to list them all would only result in my accidentally leaving some out. So to all of you with whom I have had the good fortune of sharing your knowledge I send my deepest appreciation. You are all a part of this book. A special thanks goes to a good friend and writing partner, Tom Bentz, for taking his valuable time to read the manuscript and make suggestions. Most of all, I thank my wife Donna and our two children Jordanna and Meredith for their patience and support. I dedicate this book to them.

Neil Heller, 1989

1 The Foundation of the System

THE TELEVISION SYSTEM

In its most basic form, television consists of black-and-white pictures that are made up of patterns of varying contrast. More complex systems allow the addition of color information.

Our television system starts when light falls on specific points of an optical electronic converter in the video camera, usually an image pickup tube. (To simplify our discussion, we will relate this process only to the reproduction of a black-and-white picture.) The image pickup tube transfers the incoming incident light into an electronic signal. Differences in the frequencies of the incoming light result in amplitude differences in the electronic signal, which create contrast or brightness changes. These changes of contrast appear to our eyes as details.

The camera output signal will probably be recorded on tape and the tape edited. In the end, however, the electronic signal will be transmitted by a cable or, as in broadcast television, the signal will be converted back into an optical representation displaying the same contrast patterns of the original signal. Similar to a film projector with its sprockets that separate each frame of film, continuous viewable transmission of the individual television frames is ensured by the synchronized scanning of the reading beam of the camera and the writing beam of the viewing monitor.

Sync

Synchronization (sync), an essential element of the television system, permits the transmission of continuous pictures from the transmission point of the TV signal to the reception point. Without consistent sync, a television system will not operate.

How the System Uses Sync

The reference sync of a system is usually taken from the camera. Within the camera, sync is generated from a single (integrated circuit) generator. The sync is processed and used to drive the deflection circuits of the camera which, in turn, are responsible for directing the scanning beam. At this point, the signal is a combination of active video scan and a blanking-like signal. In the final steps of signal processing within the camera sync, the blanking and subcarrier frequencies are added.

The videotape recorder generates no sync of its own. The speed of the video head and movement of the tape are tied to the incoming reference. While the sync coming from the camera is extremely stable, the playback sync from the recorder is not. How closely the videotape recorder playback sync approximates that of the camera is dependent on the time base stability of the recorder.

Scanning

Scanning is the process by which the picture is divided into a number of horizontal and vertical lines. In the camera, the scan begins at the top of the picture and is drawn horizontally across the faceplate of the tube as it reads one horizontal line of information. In the monitor, the beam writes this information as one line across the picture tube. The sync pulse signal of the television system ensures that the reading and writing stay in step with each other. In this way, the placement of the elements between camera and monitor correspond with one another.

In the United States, the standard television signal is created by an electronic beam that scans the picture tube at a rate of 525 lines of picture information, 30 times each second. This is known as the NTSC (National Television Standards Committee) system.

An image repetition rate of 30 frames per second is low enough to be detected by the human eye, and the image would appear to flicker. For this reason, the television system uses two interlaced fields which effectively doubles the frequency of picture occurrence to 60 pictures per second and eliminates any visible flicker. Each field contains 262.5 horizontal lines of which 241.5 represent video information. The remaining 21 lines are used to blank out video information and allow the beam to reposition itself at the top of the screen. (See Figure 1.1.) Each field is labeled odd or even, depending on the line that starts the scan. Since the first scan line of the first field is line number one, and progresses by scanning lines 3, 5, 7, 9, etc., it is called the odd field. The next field begins with line number 2 and proceeds to fill in the information between the odd lines by scanning lines 2, 4, 6, 8, etc. In this way, the odd field is interlaced with the even. The two fields are separated by the vertical synchronization interval, which occurs 60 times per second.

THE COMPOSITE VIDEO SIGNAL

In order to understand the function of sync, it is necessary to express its relationship to video in terms of amplitude and timing measurements. The NTSC television signal is a complex combination of sine waves and pulses that carry the information necessary to create a television image. Together, this information forms the composite video signal, which consists of horizontal sync, vertical sync and video information. (See Figure 1.2.) The horizontal sync synchronizes the scanning electron beam of the TV monitor so that each line of picture information will start at the same lateral position during the scanning process. The vertical sync controls the vertical field-by-field scanning of the video camera's picture tube.

The total television signal has an amplitude of one volt from its lowest to its highest point. The first three-tenths of the volt contains the sync information. The remaining seven-tenths contains the viewable (active) video information. In terms of television measurements, volts do not offer enough accuracy for television engineers. To overcome this problem, the Institute of Radio Engineers (IRE) created a scale that is used on waveform monitors to specify the various components of the television wave form. (See Figure 1.3.) The complete signal is contained within IRE units ranging from −40 to +100. Video information

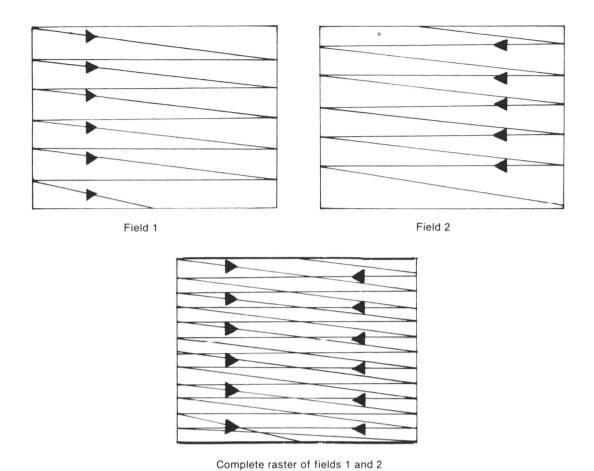

Field 1   Field 2

Complete raster of fields 1 and 2

Figure 1.1: Interlaced Scanning.

ranges from 0 to +100 IRE and equates to 0.714 volts. Sync and other non-image signals are located between 0 and −40 IRE units.

The Blanking Interval

Each field of video contains 241.5 lines of video information separated by horizontal sync signals that provide synchronization and retrace time. The total of the sync signal and time allotted for retrace is referred to as the blanking interval.

The blanking interval makes the horizontal and vertical retrace lines invisible and begins at the last section of active video, when the signal level falls to 0 IRE. The signal continues for a period of microseconds (u sec) and then drops to the −40 IRE level. This transition marks the start of the horizontal sync signal. After the sync period is over, the signal level returns to 0 IRE and remains there until the start of active video on the next horizontal line.

Timing duration and signal levels are important to the television system as they provide a means of distinguishing sync from video, as well as horizontal from vertical. Within a television picture, the level of voltage will be determined by the brightness of each part of the picture. The brighter parts of the picture will result in higher signal levels than the darker portions. Since the sync signals are reserved for levels between 0 and −40 IRE, care has

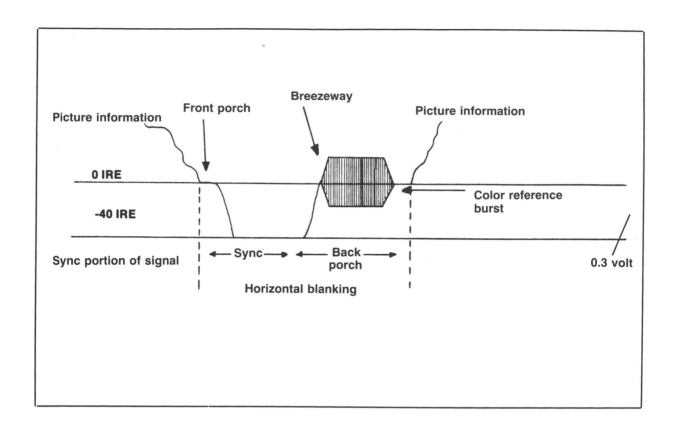

Figure 1.2: Horizontal Blanking Interval.

to be taken that the darkest parts of the picture do not result in signals that fall into this region and are mistaken for sync. (See Figure 1.4.) To prevent this, the blackest part of the picture is fixed by the camera electronics to a level of 7.5 IRE. This is referred to as the "setup" level. Since signals occurring below this setup level are darker than those contained within the active video area, the sync signals are sometimes referred to as "blacker than black." In this way (by using IRE measurements), the voltage level of each portion of the television signal is used to tell the difference between sync and video.

Timing is used to tell the difference between the horizontal and vertical intervals. The entire horizontal blanking duration occurs within a period of 11.44 u sec. Vertical blanking begins after the occurrence of 262.5 horizontal periods and is measured in milliseconds. Thus, all

components of the video chain (videotape recorders and monitors) that need to separate horizontal and vertical signals can do so by filtering networks, which make use of their distinctive timing differences.

Detailing the Composite Video Signal

Both horizontal and vertical signals have many similarities. The blanking period between the end of the active video signal where the level changes to 0 IRE, and the leading edge of sync at −40 IRE, is known as the "front porch." (See Figure 1.2.) The front porch ensures that the video picture is blanked out prior to the beginning of retrace. The transition from the front porch to the leading edge of sync is represented by a drop from 0 IRE to −40 IRE. This drop system reference is established as beam retrace occurs. During

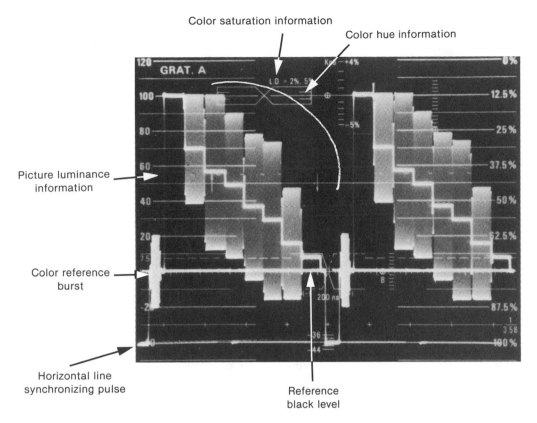

Figure 1.3: Two horizontal scan lines of the NTSC color bar signal as read on a waveform monitor. Photo courtesy Tektronix, Inc.

horizontal retrace, the beam travels from the right side to the left side of the picture. During vertical retrace, the beam travels from the bottom to the top of the picture. After retrace is over, the system must reestablish a voltage reference. This is the purpose of the "back porch" (see Figure 1.2), which occurs when the trailing edge of sync goes from − 40 IRE to 0 IRE. The back porch area of horizontal sync is also used for the transmission of the color burst signal.

At the end of the first field, the beam returns to the top of the picture to begin scanning the second field. Since the first (odd) field ends with half of a horizontal line, the next (even) field must begin with half of a horizontal line. This integration of the odd and even fields is necessary for the components of the television chain to maintain synchronization and continuity in signal transmissions.

Since the beginning of the vertical blanking period occurs after 262.5 horizontal periods, and ends after approximately 21 horizontal lines, horizontal sync continuity must be maintained throughout the vertical blanking period. Different conditions for the starting of integration could result in severe picture disturbance. In order to prevent disturbance, the occurrence of horizontal sync is doubled before, during and after vertical sync. These sync pulses are called equalizing pulses and are used to ensure a uniform transition of horizontal sync between odd and even fields.

The composite video signal is complete when sync is added to the active picture information.

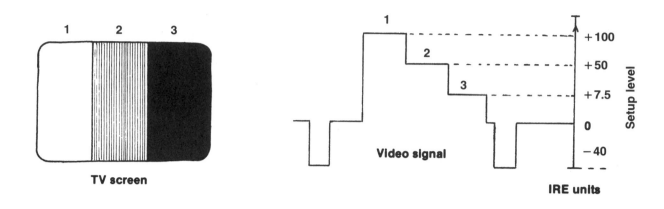

Figure 1.4: Relationship between video signal, image on TV screen and IRE units.

ADDING COLOR

Color is a complex relationship of both signal amplitude and phase. In this section, we will discuss the frequency and position of color within the horizontal signal.

The addition of color information to the television signal creates some potential problems. To begin with, color signals must be completely compatible with black-and-white monitors. Second, the addition of these signals, which contain their own amplitude, must not distort the brightness levels of the original black-and-white signal. And, finally, the frequency of the color signal must be a function of the frequency of horizontal sync.

Determining the Frequency of Color

Color information is present in two areas of the television signal. Within the horizontal blanking period, a portion of the color signal called "burst" is inserted, and used as a reference. The color information found within the active video is called "chroma" (chrominance). Both burst and chroma must be present on the horizontal line for the monitor to produce a color picture.

The Color Subcarrier

In order to be broadcast as a composite video signal, the color information is first modulated by a sinusoidal wave called the color subcarrier. The color burst and chroma portions of the composite video signal are comprised of this subcarrier.

The color subcarrier frequency (3.58 MHz) was selected so the color information would be positioned in such a way that it would not interfere with the information responsible for providing brightness (luminance) and detail (resolution).

Interleaving

If the color frequency is an integral multiple of the horizontal frequency, it will repeat every new horizontal line and will appear as a bonafide video signal. This would result in an interference pattern of dark and bright stripes corresponding to the frequency of the line in which it appears. In order to prevent this, the color subcarrier is presented as an odd multiple of one half of the frequency of horizontal sync. In this way, the harmonics of the subcarrier are found in between the harmonics of the detail (luminance) portion of the video signal, or the chroma signal is "interleaved" in the video. Interleaving is necessary so that the color and luminance information can be broadcast at the same time without interfering with each other. Signals that interleave (in the NTSC system) can be expressed as:

$$f_i = \frac{2n+1}{2} \times f_H$$

Where: f_1 = signals which interleave;
$2n + 1$ = definition of an odd number;
f_H = horizontal sync rate; and
f_{SC} = frequency of the subcarrier.

For the NTSC system, the color subcarrier has a frequency of 3.58 MHz which is the 455th harmonic on one half the line frequency. To accommodate the relationship between horizontal sync and burst, the frequency of horizontal sync changes from 60 Hz to 59.94 Hz.

Due to interleaving, the phase of the color subcarrier alternates 180 degrees from the line of the odd field to the next line of the even field. Because these signals are both of equal amplitude and opposite polarities, the subcarrier found on line one of the odd field and the subcarrier found on line two of the even field cancel each other out. Since the phase of the subcarrier found on all the lines of the even field will be the same, it is possible that this could produce interference. Therefore, to avoid interference, complete subcarrier cancellation occurs over four fields. In order to further reduce the possibility of chrominance/luminance interference, the frequency of the color subcarrier is designed to be as high as possible. Many television monitors cut off their luminance frequencies at 3 MHz to avoid interfering with the 3.58 MHz subcarrier.

The Breezeway

As noted before, the burst signal is located on the back porch of horizontal sync. It is separated from the trailing edge of sync by a small period of blanking called the "breezeway" (See Figure 1.2). Although the period of the breezeway is the shortest of all the signals within the horizontal blanking period, lasting only 0.381 u sec, it prevents the first cycle of burst from occurring at the same time as the trailing edge of sync. If this separation is lost, the voltage reference between the leading and trailing edges of sync would cause an overall brightness change in the picture.

Like sync, the burst signal has an amplitude of 0.3 volts. In order to maintain the voltage reference level of the back porch, each half of the burst signal is located above and below the 0 IRE level. The television system averages the equal positive and negative transitions and recognizes the burst as having a 0 level.

The burst signal, as well as the amplitude and widths of the rest of the components of horizontal and vertical blanking, are measured on a waveform monitor. Subcarrier phase is measured on a vectorscope.

SYNC STANDARDS

The current standards for transmitting television signals are set by the Federal Communications Commission (FCC), and are referred to as RS-170. These standards define all individual pulse widths and amplitudes contained within horizontal and vertical blanking. Regardless of overall picture quality, which is unregulated and determined only by the condition of the equipment used, sync must remain constant. With the possible exception of "live" news bulletin broadcasts, all television transmissions originate from videotape recorders. Due to the mechanical design of these recorders, the resulting sync is subject to the inconsistencies of the tape transport.

These inconsistencies translate to a playback sync rate that is not steady—it varies. A video signal with a varying sync rate cannot be used in conjunction with any other steady video signal—it must be made steady first. In order to achieve this, a time base corrector (TBC) is used. This device corrects the varying sync rate (called "time base") so that a VTR can be used with other video sources.

Additional processing can cause the expansion of the blanking widths. Since both monitors and television sets expect to see no more than the highest limits of permissible blanking (11.44 u secs of horizontal blanking and 21 horizontal lines of vertical blanking), this expansion of blanking causes them to replace video in the active scan. Since this affects the faster duration horizontal rate signals first, a black bar would appear at the left side of the screen.

In the mid-1970s the FCC, supporting the growth of electronic news gathering (ENG), permitted the "occasional" transmission of videotapes with over-the-limit blanking widths. By 1978, however, these oversights were becoming so commonplace that the FCC issued a public notice informing broadcasters that a "Notice of Violation" would be issued for all transmissions in excess of 12 u sec of horizontal blanking and 23 horizontal lines of vertical blanking.

Specification RS-170A

Broadcast engineers, who were responsible for the materials transmitted by their stations, expressed similar concerns. Many television stations would not accept tapes if their blanking widths exceeded 10.8 u secs and 20 horizontal lines. Broadcasters, acting through the Electronics Industries Group, drafted a tentative television sync specification called RS-170A. This specification not only dealt with the excesses of blanking, but also called for a constant subcarrier for the horizontal timing phase relationship. This was important because changes in the horizontal phase relationship can result in color hue shifts. The proposed standard called for a fixed 5.3 ± 0.1 u sec horizontal sync to burst timing relationship over each of the four color fields. Although no official action was ever taken by the FCC, the advent of highly accurate sync generators (most often in the form of integrated circuits) enabled equipment manufacturers to respond to the needs of the industry.

When considering the type of sync required to transmit a signal, it is important to remember that FCC rules apply only to those signals transmitted over the air for *commercial* use. This includes network and local transmissions which can be received by television sets. Any signals transmitted by cable, including those which are received by satellite (such as HBO, Showtime and ESPN) are regulated by standards set by the chief engineer of each station. Quite often, no particular attention is given to standards for the transmission of programming provided by a cable company's local origination or public access channels. This type of programming is usually provided by members of the local community and is shot on low-cost consumer equipment.

OTHER COUNTRIES, OTHER SYSTEMS

The NTSC system, which is used in the United States, is found basically in countries that use a 60 cycle alternating current per second power source. This accounts for the relationship of 30 frames per second made from 60 fields per second. Most countries, however, have a power line frequency of 50 Hz, instead of 60 Hz. Black-and-white only (monochrome) signals are transmitted at a 25 frame/50 field per second rate. In addition, 625 scanning lines are used as opposed to the 525 lines for NTSC.

These countries use a different color system known as Phase Alternation each Line (PAL) or Sequential Colors with Memory (SECAM). Of these two systems, PAL is the most commonly used and most resembles our own NTSC. The subcarrier used is 4.43 MHz and the phase alternating method is so stable that PAL receivers don't require tint or hue controls. The SECAM receiver also has freedom from automatic phase controlled circuits typically found in NTSC receivers. Americans traveling abroad notice the increased color phase stability and greater saturation.

The important factor is that these systems are *not* interchangeable. Recordings made on a PAL recorder cannot be played back on an NTSC recorder. To begin with, the different rates of picture taking, 30 frames per second for NTSC and 25 frames for PAL and SECAM, cause the playback of the PAL tape on an NTSC recorder to show a condition similar to a loss of horizontal hold on the monitor. Of course, all color is lost as the NTSC receiver cannot recognize the 4.43 MHz color burst. Conversion from one standard to another is possible only with the use of expensive conversion equipment found at better-equipped production and duplication houses. Likewise, cameras and recorders with different systems cannot be mixed.

Part 1
Videotape Recorders

2 Videotape Recorders: Determining Needs

Purchasing a videotape recorder is no different than purchasing any other type of product. Your needs will probably be tempered by the amount of dollars you have to spend. Needs and dollars will be the two major factors that will determine the type of equipment you purchase. But, before you begin to look at specification sheets, you should ask yourself some basic questions that will help you to determine what your needs are. These include:

- What are your goals?
- What type of productions will you be shooting?
- What kind (quality) of finished product do you want?
- Where will you be doing most of your production work—in the field or in the studio?

If your production requires editing and post-production, for example, you will have to determine which type of equipment will be used most often, and which should be reserved for rental. A portable deck can be used for both studio and field production, while a player/recorder usually requires the use of an AC power source which limits its usage to indoor applications. If your production requirements include editing, the question to ask is: How often will you be editing? The most basic editing systems range in price from $6000 to $9000. Comparable systems usually rent for about $35 to $50 per hour. If your editing and post-production requirements will be 200 hours during your first (and most important) year, your money might be better spent on the rental of good post-production equipment. Equipment such as image enhancers can vastly improve the quality of production of the equipment used for the original shooting. On the other hand, if your budget is limited to the purchase of one major type of recorder, and doesn't allow much room for rentals, you might consider the purchase of a full-featured stand-alone editor which can accept any type of video input.

Always consider the purchase of a piece of video equipment as part of a total system. The building of your system starts with the purchase of your initial piece of equipment such as a camera or a VTR. Since most equipment has a life span of approximately five to seven years, it is necessary to plan the future growth of your system with regard to your future production requirements.

VIDEOTAPE FORMATS

Questions regarding the future growth, direction and quality of your system usually center around the subject of format.

In today's world of rapidly advancing technology, the introduction of new videotape formats seems to be increasing at a rate greater than the improvement of existing ones. And, more often than not, the choice of a format is based on the availability of capital, and future growth is not taken into consideration. Present availability of a certain type of format does not necessarily mean that it has gained industry acceptance. Lack of industry acceptance will often mean a sharp future devaluation of your equipment along with increased difficulty in obtaining service and spare parts.

The method of distribution for your programming will also play a large role in determining your choice of format. You must determine who will be viewing your production and the format of the equipment they will use for viewing—1/2-inch, 3/4-inch, 8mm, etc. During the production and duplication processes, signal quality will be lost if you tape in one format and distribute in another.

Another consideration in the selection of format is compatibility. In other words, you will have to select a format that will enable you to utilize the same type of equipment for each aspect of your production. This is particularly true if you intend to rely on equipment rentals to complete your production. Most full-service video dealerships have editing facilities. It is a good idea to make sure you can directly edit your tapes with the same format you're using for the shoot. Chances are, if you cannot find editing services in the format you are considering, then that format has probably not been widely accepted.

Formats are usually classified by quality of signal, features and common form of usage (broadcast, industrial, consumer). They are listed in Table 2.1.

Table 2.1: Videotape Formats

Classification	Common Formats
Broadcast	1-inch Type C 1/2-inch M Format 1/2-inch Betacam®
Industrial	3/4-inch U-Matic 1/2-inch VHS 1/2-inch Beta S-VHS
Consumer	1/2-inch VHS 1/2-inch Beta 8mm S-VHS

BROADCAST VIDEO

In strictly technical terms, the word *Broadcast* means that the signals reproduced by the videotape conform to the RS-170 sync specifications set by the FCC. Regardless of the classification of the recorder, two conditions must exist for a tape to air. First, since the recorded signal is basically a reflection of the input signal, it must conform to broadcast standards. Next, playback from any format of tape is subject to instability due to its mechanical transport. Therefore, all recorder playback material must be processed through a time base corrector (TBC) in order to stabilize the sync. If we apply these two conditions to any format of recording, the playback signal can be aired. Taking these factors into consideration, the term *Broadcast* has come to mean the highest possible quality of signal.

In broadcast, the playback signal has the highest signal-to-noise ratio and horizontal resolution. In order to achieve this, 1-inch and 1/2-inch VHS M formats and Betacam®

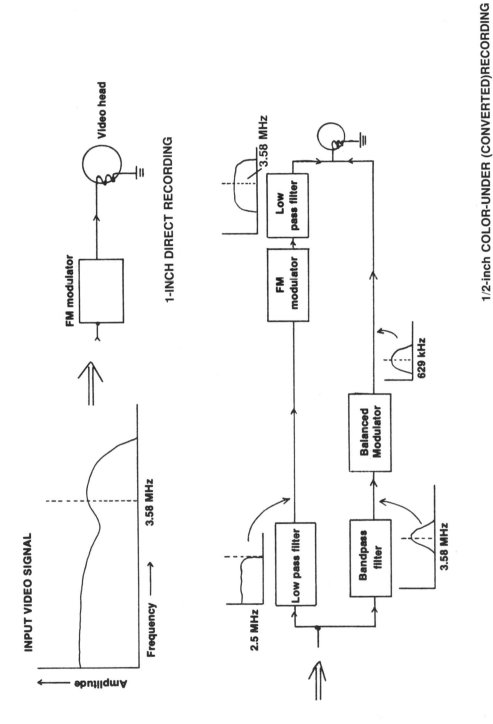

Figure 2.1: Comparison of direct and color-under recording methods.

employ a direct recording method that maintains the original characteristics, specifically the bandwidth, of the input signal. In electronics, signals processed at high bandwidths contain more details than signals limited to lower bandwidths. By not altering the bandwidth of the input signal, particularly the 3.58 MHz subcarrier, 1-inch recorders are capable of reproducing between 400 to 500 horizontal lines of resolution. The 1/2-inch broadcast formats achieve approximately 350 horizontal lines. This is approximately 100 to 120 lines greater than industrial 1/2-inch and 3/4-inch recorders.

INDUSTRIAL VIDEO

The industrial formats convert their input signals to a limited range of frequencies. The color subcarrier is converted down below 1 MHz. During this conversion process, additional noise is added to the signal thereby lowering the signal-to-noise ratio and horizontal resolution (see Figure 2.1).

3/4-Inch U-Matic

The oldest currently existing industrial format is the 3/4-inch U-Matic. This format was introduced to the market approximately 15 years ago by the Sony Corporation. Due to its pricing (which was far below other types of recorders available at the time), its ease of operation (the videotape was housed in a cassette) and the ability of the recorder to self thread, the 3/4-inch U-Matic format was able to become one of the first universally accepted formats. Although it has been challenged by the rapid growth of the 1/2-inch industrial recorders, many manufacturers still feel that regardless of the method of distribution employed, many users still prefer to do their primary production on U-Matic recorders.

1/2-Inch Videotape: Industrial and Consumer

In terms of the growth of the video industry no single product has become a better symbol

than the 1/2-inch videotape recorder. Home use of 1/2-inch recorders laid the foundation for the growth of the industrial 1/2-inch marketplace. As noted before, the term *industrial video* commonly meant that the production and distribution of the program was done on 3/4-inch U-Matic. While many corporations have maintained or even expanded their use of 3/4-inch equipment for original production and post-production editing, the 1/2-inch format has become the principal method for the distribution of corporate programming.

The primary advantage 1/2-inch has over 3/4-inch is price. Prices are lower in every category of function for players, recorders and editors. This low pricing combined with high quality has created an expansion in the use of videotape recorders. The 1/2-inch industrial videotape recorders have given birth to the so-called "wedding crowd producers," those amateur television directors who make extra money on the weekends shooting weddings and birthday parties. Prior to this, the costs of taping and editing such productions on 3/4-inch equipment priced them out of the marketplace. Much of local organization and public access cable programming has been built on the cornerstone of 1/2-inch industrial units.

Since the specifications of 1/2-inch recorders come very close to those of 3/4-inch and, in turn, consumer 1/2-inch recorder specifications are close to those of their industrial counterparts, the definitions of industrial and consumer are often confused. Industrial has come to mean that a recorder's performance, in terms of signal-to-noise ratio and horizontal resolution, is the best possible within that particular format.

When talking about the 1/2-inch format, manufacturers have some very particular definitions of industrial units. The first is based on distribution rather than the recorder itself. Industrial units are distributed by a select group of dealers whose aims center more around a system concept than moving individual bulk items. These dealers are well equipped to determine applications needs and usually can provide repair services at their locations.

Another difference between the industrial

and consumer 1/2-inch formats, as pointed out by manufacturers, is the use of heavy-duty components and the emphasis on chassis strength in the industrial units. This can be particularly important when considering the purchase of a portable unit. A final consideration is accurate, noise-free and variable function editing usually found only on the 1/2-inch industrial units.

THE PRINCIPLES OF RECORDING

The primary goal behind the design of any videotape recorder is the reproduction of a signal that resembles the original input video as closely as possible. The key factors that determine the quality of the playback signal are the specifications of the video recorder's resolution and signal-to-noise ratio. The analog process of magnetic recording limits the exact reproduction of the incoming video signal. The degree of accuracy of signal reproduction is related to the method of recording used. This, in turn, accounts for the different recording formats used in video production.

The principle behind videotape recording is the same as that employed in audiotape recording. Video information is applied to the tape by means of a small electromagnet—the video head. The individual poles of this magnet are positioned close together but they do not touch. The video signal, as applied to the head, can be thought of as an alternating current (AC), having a positive and negative cycle. As this AC signal flows through the coils of the video head it causes a magnetic field to develop between the two poles of the head. As the AC swings positive the magnetic field begins its build up. As the cycle goes negative the field collapses. This changing state of magnetism is referred to as flux. Since the rise and fall of the magnetic flux matches that of the amplitude of the incoming video it can be used to impress itself on an oxide-coated surface such as videotape. The result of tape-to-head contact is a section of tape that has magnetic flux equal to the direction and intensity of the video signal.

The method of alternating magnetic flux lines to record video brings us to our first limitation in signal reproduction.

Writing Speeds

Since flux is composed of changing polarity, tape speed must be fast enough to allow ample room on the tape so the complete signal cycle can be recorded. If the tape speed is too slow, the transition between the positive and negative part of the cycle will occur at the same point on the tape. As a result, no signal will be recorded at all. If we wish to increase the ability of the recorder to record and playback high resolution signals, we must increase the tape speed.

We face a similar problem when passing high frequency signals through the video head and on to the tape. As noted previously, the signal is recorded on the tape when energy in the form of magnetic flux is transferred between the gap in the video head. If the physical gap of the head is big enough to allow the complete cycle of the signal to pass, the resulting energy would be zero. Therefore, to ensure that the maximum amount of energy is transferred to the tape, the head gap width must be equal to, or less than, one half the shortest wavelength you wish to record. At this physical gap size, only the positive or negative portion of the cycle will be present in the gap at any given time.

The highest energy transfer in the *head gap* can be expressed as the following formula:

$$\text{head gap} = \frac{\text{wavelength}}{2}$$

In turn, *wavelength* can be expressed as:

velocity (head-to-tape speed)

$$\text{wavelength} = \frac{\text{velocity}}{\text{highest recorded frequency}}$$

Velocity is the speed at which the tape makes contact with the video head. This term is also known as the *writing speed* as it expresses the rate at which the signal is written on the tape.

By combining the head gap and the tape speed, we come up with the following formula:

$$\text{head gap} = \frac{\text{writing speed}}{2 \times \text{highest frequency}}$$

In order to obtain the highest allowable recording frequency, the head gap size must decrease, or the writing speed must increase. Faster writing speeds allow for larger head gap sizes, while slower writing speeds necessitate smaller head gaps. Broadcast recorders record and playback high frequency (resolution) signals because they employ high writing speeds with proportionally large head gaps. As such, they can record all the signals of the incoming video without any change.

The tape speeds required to record a full bandwidth video signal consume a great deal of tape, and the electronics needed to maintain stable recording are costly. This is the main problem with broadcast quality recorders—the ability to record and play back high quality equals high cost.

Both industrial and consumer users of video require less costly methods for recording video. This means slower recording speeds for less tape consumption. U-Matic, 3/4-inch and 1/2-inch VHS and Beta formats are designed to fill these needs. However, trade off in cost is followed by trade off in performance. Increases in recording time in U-Matic and consumer recorders result in losses in recording and playback frequency response. These losses can only be made up to a limited degree by decreasing the size of the video head gap (see Figure 2.2). As a result, in order to accommodate all the components found in the video signal, it is necessary to compress the signal into a band of frequencies capable of being recorded. This conversion process used in 3/4-inch and 1/2-inch industrial/consumer products results in a loss of resolution and signal-to-noise ratio compared to broadcast systems which "direct record" the incoming video.

Frequency Response

The key to the engineering differences between each category of recording is the relationship between frequency response and writing speed. Frequency response changes dramatically between 1-inch SMPTE Type C formats at the upper end of the broadcast recording spectrum and long duration consumer recorders at the lower end. (For example, broadcast, 1-inch is 0 MHz to 4.2 MHz; MII, Betcam SP is 0 MHz to 4.5 MHz; and VHS, 3/4-inch is 0 MHz to 3 MHz.)

Writing speeds for 1-inch units run at approximately 1000 ips (inches per second), while consumer units equal approximately a quarter of that rate. Within the video spectrum, signals exist between a frequency range of 30 Hz, which represents sync; 3.58 MHz, which represents the color information; and 4.2 MHz, which represents the whitest portion of the video signal. This is commonly referred to as a full-width signal, since it represents the maximum bandwidth the current U.S. television system is capable of transmitting over the air. High writing speeds enable recorders to reproduce high frequencies, which hold greater detail.

Signal-to-Noise Ratio

Another advantage of recording high writing speeds is the resulting higher ratio of signal to noise in the playback picture. By "directly" recording original signals found in the incoming video onto the tape, the signal is subject to less processing (which produces additional noise). To understand why, let's take a closer look at the process of recording and playing back signals on 3/4-inch and 1/2-inch videotape recorders.

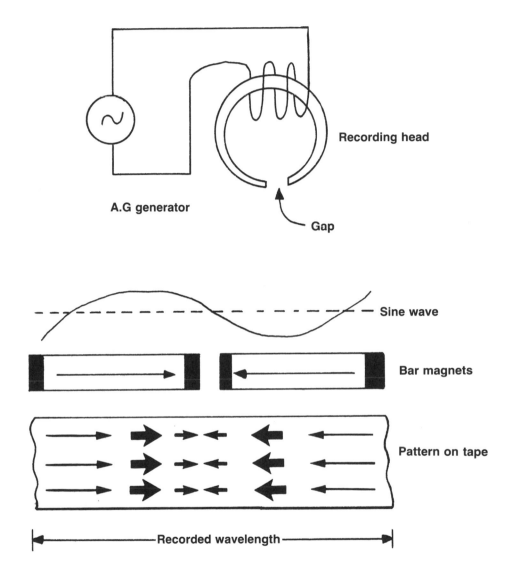

Figure 2.2: Head gap and recorded wavelength.

Converted Subcarrier Recording

As noted before, longer recording durations result in losses of writing speed, which are only partially made up by reductions in head gap size. As a result, it is impossible for full-bandwidth frequencies to be recorded directly onto tape. In order to record video on 3/4-inch and 1/2-inch tape, the signal must be converted to a bandwidth that can be properly handled by the format system. This method is known as converted subcarrier recording. During this process the color portion of the signal is separated from the luminance and converted from 3.58 MHz to a frequency below 1 MHz. This also results in a reduction of the color bandwidth. In order to separate chrominance from luminance, filtering is necessary, which in itself reduces the high frequency content of the luminance. The result of this loss of bandwidth is a loss of detail or resolution. Since 3/4-inch recorders have higher writing speeds than 1/2-inch units, their bandwidths are approximately 60% greater than those of 1/2-inch recorders. Due to this increased bandwidth, the number of horizontal lines 3/4-inch recorders can reproduce is somewhat greater than that of 1/2-inch. The overall figures are approximately: 250 horizontal lines in the color playback of a 3/4-inch recorder, compared to 230 horizontal lines for a 1/2-inch recorder. (S-VHS has more than 400 horizontal lines.)

Higher writing speeds provide a greater signal-to-noise ratio in the playback picture. The conversion process used to record signals on 3/4-inch and 1/2-inch videotape must be converted back by an RF modulator so the signal can be reproduced on a video monitor or regular television. This additional signal processing adds noise to the video signal and detracts from picture quality. Since the conversion process used for both 3/4-inch and 1/2-inch recorders is similar, there is no great difference in their playback signal-to-noise ratio. This figure is approximately 45db (decibels) compared to 48db for 1-inch units. Although

3db may not seem like much of a difference, the decibel scale is logarithmic, and counts on the order of tens. Therefore, recorders having higher number db signal-to-noise ratios will produce better pictures.

The generations of recordings that result from both tape editing, and dubbing signal-to-noise ratio and resolution, fall off rapidly. For this reason, even if the final method of distribution for your programming is limited to 1/2-inch consumer units, the original production, as well as post-production editing, should be done on the equipment offering the best signal characteristics.

THE MIDDLE GROUND: BROADCAST 1/2-INCH RECORDING SYSTEMS

While 1/2-inch VHS and Beta equipment provide a solution to the problems of cost and portability for the consumer and low-end industrial marketplaces, they do not provide acceptable quality for broadcast and high-end industrial users.

One-inch equipment produces the needed quality, but at great expense, and its weight and bulk make it unusable for portable applications. (Figure 2.3 illustrates a rare 1-inch portable recorder.) Even 3/4-inch recorders, which for approximately 15 years have been the most popular format for electronic news gathering, have not been improved upon to the satisfaction of broadcasters and producers who require good video reproduction after multiple generations. And, there is the camera-to-VCR connector cable, which not only is a source of unreliability, but requires additional technical personnel just to hook it up correctly.

The Camcorder

By maintaining the physical characteristics of the 1/2-inch formats, both Sony (Beta) and Panasonic/Matsushita (VHS) have been able to answer the problems of size and wiring by combining the recording mechanisms with the camera. The result is commonly referred to as

Figure 2.3: Rare 1-inch portable videotape recorder.

a camcorder. The problem of performance still exists, and the answer as always is to increase the bandwidth via higher writing speeds. These result in color playback resolutions of approximately 350 horizontal lines. These faster writing speeds are the reasons why both the Beta and VHS formats, when used in their broadcast configurations have considerably shorter recording times than their consumer counterparts. For both VHS and Beta standard cassettes, T-120 and L-750 respectively, the recording time is limited to 20 minutes. Second generation recorders (MII, Betacam SP) have extended recording time up to 90 minutes due to the use of metal tape and larger cassettes.

Recording Color Information

Aside from the format differences that have existed since these products were introduced

in their consumer versions, the broadcast products have differences in the way they record color information. Sony's Betacam® and Panasonic's MII use a compressed time division multiplex system that compresses the primary colors of red and blue, in the form of R-Y and B-Y (where R = red, B = blue and Y = luminance), into a single video track, while maintaining the needed bandwidth. This system is possible because the bandwidth requirements for the two color video signals each equal less than one half that of the luminance signal. By delaying each of the color signals they can be multiplexed into one video track.

Quality After Multiple Generations

The manufacturers talk about the advantages of each of these systems (Beta vs. VHS) with regard to the quality of playback picture after multiple generations. It is up to the user to choose the format he prefers.

Under most production situations the original tape will be subject to editing after which the tape will become the master for future dubbing. As a result, the edited master must have the best quality. If you are going to be dubbing with anything else than a first generation tape, the major concern will be the end quality after multiple generations.

Aside from picture quality, high-end industrial and broadcast units have features that separate them from their consumer counterparts. These features enable the user to create end products with a greater degree of accuracy and versatility. Such features include: dual audio tracks, time code and external sync and subcarrier.

Dual Audio Tracks

Dual audio tracks allow for the recording of two separate audio sources. With the continued development of stereo television, particularly in the area of music production, and bilingual industrial tapes, the need for stereo production is expected to increase. In addition, users can take advantage of a recorder's dual capability by using the second audio channel to record time code.

Time Code

Time code is a signal recorded along with the video that gives each recorded frame a unique code or address. During editing, controllers with the ability to read this code can edit accurately within one frame.

External Sync and Subcarrier

Usually, the video recorder is part of an overall video system in which an external device, such as time base corrector, is used. The time base corrector stabilizes the playback signal from the video recorder by referencing it to fixed external sync and subcarrier signals. This is important for a number of reasons. First, it allows the playback signal to be mixed with other input sources such as cameras and other recorders. Second, by stabilizing the recorder's playback signal, its quality is increased.

Since the speed of the playback tape is not constant due to inconsistencies in tape transport mechanisms, the sync signals, particularly those responsible for maintaining good color reproduction, are constantly in a state of change. As a result of these changes in sync, the phase, or hue, of the playback color changes. These changes are transferred during dubbing, and the problem is further compounded by the transport of the recording videotape recorder. For this reason, color reproduction is the first quality to suffer during multiple generation recordings. Stabilizing the playback signal via a time base corrector helps to maintain good picture quality for edited and dubbed tapes.

CHOOSING THE RECORDER

The videotape recording industry has seen its greatest changes over the past five years. Technology continues to provide improved means of recording to the user. These advances have also created an additional set of problems as all types of users seek not the ultimate recorder, but a grouping of units that share both common formats and components. Format compatibility has been a greater problem than that of performance. Lack of format compatibility means that the user cannot be assured of long-term manufacturer support as well as future equipment value. As we have noted, only Type C 1-inch and 3/4-inch formats offer such compatibility, but at the expense of technology and price that reflect their age.

Future format standardization is unclear as manufacturers are unwilling to compromise their positions. Broadcast standard committees, such as the Society of Motion Picture and

Television Engineers (SMPTE), have failed to reach agreement on standard specifications for 1/2-inch and 1/4-inch tape formats.

Advances in the Industrial and Broadcast Fields

Even within existing formats there is change.

3/4-Inch SP

Sony took the conventional 3/4-inch format a step further by slightly increasing the FM carrier frequency without destroying compatibility. This enhanced version of the 3/4-inch format is called 3/4-inch SP. While it represents an effort to keep the 3/4-inch format appealing and to strengthen its market, SP recorded tapes will not produce significantly better results in a conventional machine. Superior playback results occur only if SP recorded tapes are played in SP machines.

MII

MII is a metamorphosized M format; however, MII and M are not compatible. MII utilizes the Y, R-Y and B-Y color video signals, time compression FM recording and metal particle tape. In MII, FM audio for high fidelity is standard with the option for digital audio. With these features and performance, MII meets 1-inch. The MII format also includes a camcorder model, as well as a complete range of studio and field recorders and editors.

Betacam SP®

Betacam SP® is a competitor to MII. With improvements such as shifted FM carrier frequencies, the Betacam SP® improves upon the Betacam® format indicating that there is some compatibility between the SP units and Betacam® models.

Super VHS

The S-VHS format uses a T-120 VHS cassette and records in the pre-existing two-hour SP and extended play six-hour EP modes. The cassette itself uses an improved magnetic material which is capable of recording high density signals. The resulting recording produces a 400 horizontal line color playback signal, almost doubling the resolution of standard VHS recorders. The format has the potential of closing the gap between consumer and industrial formats, leading to two categories; consumer and broadcast. Each of these formats would be distinguished only by its ability to maintain first generation quality through multiple generation dubs.

Is There An End in Sight?

Not only do format wars exist at the time of this writing, but we are able to predict their occurrence as developments and technological advances are made. Already, the Koreans have proposed the 4mm format and Nippon Electric Company (NEC) has offered solid state recording. Digital recording, however, is thought to be the plateau on which video recording will rest since a worldwide digital format has already been agreed upon.

On the consumer side, the advent of 8mm, supported by Sony and with a universally accepted format, may signal the beginning of the end of VHS and Beta. As uniformity comes to this consumer format, the industrial recorder version will follow.

The factors affecting the choice of a recorder are complicated by the uncertainty of format standardization. What if any of these formats will triumph as the future standard is anyone's guess.

3 Videotape Recorder Operations

In this chapter we will review some of the connections, operations, controls and common problems encountered in the operation of videotape recorders. This chapter is intended to be used as a guide. For specifics on particular models refer to the recorder's operations manual. (For information about recorders used within editing systems see Chapter 4.)

VIDEOTAPE RECORDER DIFFERENCES

All videotape recorders are parts of systems that require input signals and monitors to receive the outputs. The quality of the VCR's performance is dependent upon the quality of the system in which it operates. While all recorders require input and output connections, the types of connections used, the method of recording and playback, and the available controls differ from recorder to recorder. The number of inputs, outputs and controls available for any recorder, regardless of format, is usually in direct proportion to the cost of the recorder. For this reason, recorders can be classified into three categories: consumer, industrial and system recorders (those used within editing systems).

Consumer Recorders

Consumer recorders are usually used for basic recording from internal tuners with playback through television sets. Being the least expensive type of recorders, consumer machines contain the least number of input and output connections, and operator controls.

Industrial Recorders

Industrial recorders offer an increased number of input and output connectors. Input and output signals from these machines are usually restricted to direct sources. Playback requires the use of a monitor instead of a television set.

System Recorders

System recorders contain special inputs, outputs and operating controls that allow for increased processing of audio and video signals.

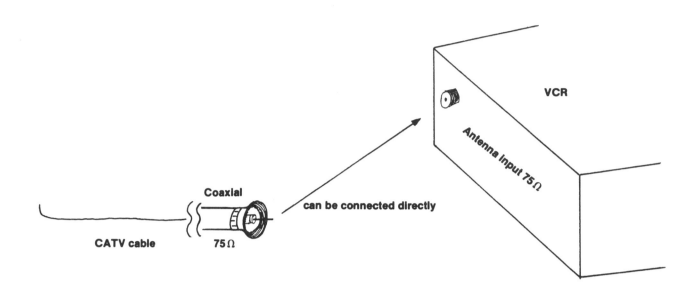

Figure 3.1: Antenna (RF) connection to the VCR.

The additional input and output connectors allow this type of recorder to be used as part of any editing system.

CONNECTORS

Each recording system requires different types of connectors. Connector requirements are determined by the types of signals to be handled.

The F Connector

F Connectors are used for inputting and outputting RF signals that are received via a television antenna and transmitted to a television set on an unused channel. This type of connector is usually only found in consumer recorders containing tuner sections.

The RCA Phone Jack

The RCA phone jack can be used as either an audio or video connector. Similar to the RF connector, it is usually found on consumer units.

The BNC Connector

The BNC connector is used for inputting and outputting video signals. It is usually found on industrial recorders.

The EIAJ 8-Pin Connector

The Electronic Industrial Association of Japan (EIAJ) 8-pin connector combines all the audio and video input and output connections on a single system connector. Its use greatly simplifies connection between recorder and monitor.

The XLR Audio Connector

The XLR audio connector is usually associated with high-end and industrial video recorders. Unlike the RCA phone jack, which carries the audio signals on a single wire, the XLR connector carries audio along two wires. This type of audio transmission is known as "balanced line audio." Balanced audio systems allow for a greater degree of audio fidelity than that found in unbalanced audio systems. However, in order to output or input a balanced audio signal, the recorder must have an internal audio transformer as part of its audio circuitry. Since this is an expensive component, its usage increases the cost of the recorder. Recorder XLR audio inputs and outputs can be used for either microphone or line level signals.

RECORDING TELEVISION SIGNALS

In order to record off-the-air television signals, a VCR must have an on-board television tuner. The incoming signal from the television antenna can be connected directly to the RF input of the recorder. Only the signal from the antenna is matched to that of the input of the recorder. (See Figure 3.1.)

Connector Cables

Connectors receive their signals from coaxial cables which transmit television signals along a center conductor surrounded by a ground shield. Coaxial cable has a characteristic impedance of 75 ohms.

Signal impedance is the resistance offered by the cable against the video signal. In order to achieve the maximum, undistorted transfer· of signals between the outputs and inputs of electronic devices, the impedances between the two must be equal. Mismatches of impedance between signal outputs and inputs will cause signal loss and distortion.

CONNECTING THE RECORDER'S RF OUTPUT

The RF output of the consumer recorder closely follows that of the recorder's input. Unlike the RF input, the output connections must meet two requirements. First, all of the antenna signals must be passed to the television receiver so that broadcast television stations can be viewed when the videotape recorder is not in use. Second, the television set must be able to receive the RF output of the recorder in order to view playback signals. The former requires that the recorder UHF signal input be coupled to the output without any signal impedance change. The VHF signal exits the recorder via an RF output F connector. (See Figure 3.2.)

Testing Connections

In order to test your connections, locate the recorder's RF converter switch, which is usually located on the back of the recorder. This switch selects the output RF channel that will be used to transmit the signal to the television set. The choice is between Channel 3 and Channel 4. Set the RF switch to the "unused" channel in your viewing area. This will prevent broadcast television transmissions from interfering with those of the recorder. Set the television receiver to the same channel you selected on the RF converter. Play back a videotape you know has a good recording and fine tune the receiver for the best picture. Almost all VCRs today contain internal electronic tuning and will automatically switch to the tuner input if nothing is connected to the video input when the recorder is in either the stop or record mode. This is known as the electronics to electronics (E to E) mode because the recorder is displaying its input via its electronics. Press each one of the channel select buttons

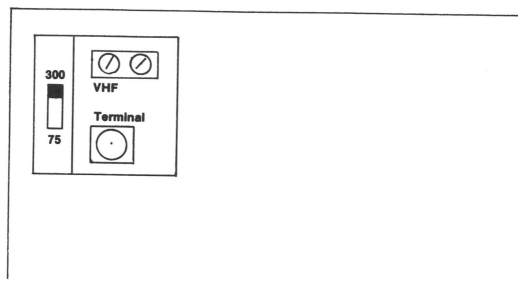

Figure 3.2: Antenna connections on a TV set.

and fine tune for best reception of the selected channel.

Since each recorder's tuner is different, it is best to follow the particular model's operating instructions. If you are inputting an RF signal directly from a cable, you will not be able to receive all the available channels, unless the recorder's tuner has more than 83-channel capability. Recording premium, or pay cable channels, will require running the cable television line through a decoder box, since these services are usually scrambled. (See Figure 3.3.)

INPUTTING VIDEO SIGNALS

All categories of recorders have video input connections. These inputs can be used to record signals from a camera or another recorder. The video input to the recorder can be made with either an RCA or BNC connector. Either type of input can be mixed with the use of an *adapter*.(Adapters are also used when the output connector is different from the input.)

All video inputs and outputs are impedance matched at 75 ohms. In cases where the record-

er has both video inputs and an internal tuner, connecting the video input will usually override the tuner input.

Controlling The Video Level

Consumer grade recorders automatically raise the highest video level of each horizontal line to the full video level of 0.7 volts AGC (automatic gain control). Industrial grade recorders allow the operator to select between a manual or automatic gain control level. In the manual mode, the level of the incoming video can be adjusted by the video level control. This control should be set up prior to recording by inputting a known 0.7 volt video signal and adjusting the control for 0 db (or 100%).

Video Mode Selection

Most video recorders automatically select the mode of the video signal by adjusting to the color burst signal. When the recorder is operated in this manner, any distortion in the phase and/or amplitude of the burst signal can

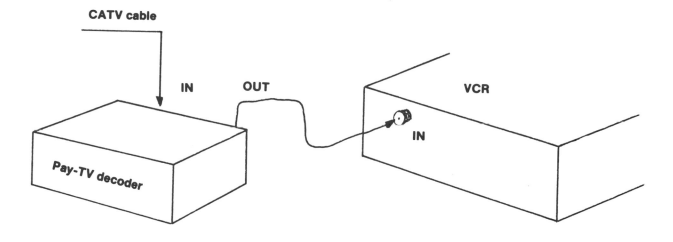

Figure 3.3: Pay-TV decoder box.

cause the recorder to switch between the color and black-and-white modes. Each time the recorder switches, there is a flash in the output picture as the signal is switched between the two different routes. In order to prevent this, industrial 3/4-inch recorders contain a video mode selector switch that can force the recorder into the black-and-white mode. Normally, this selector is set in the auto (automatic) position.

OUTPUTTING THE VIDEO SIGNAL

The video signal can be outputted from the recorder by connecting the recorder's video output to the video input of the monitor. Many new monitors can also receive normal television transmissions. These monitor/receivers have input select switches, which can be used to receive broadcast television transmissions, or the line input from a video recorder. When the video-only monitor has both a single video input connector and an EIAJ standard connector, the monitor position will represent the input from the 8-pin connector, and the line position will represent the input from the coaxial cable.

RECORDING AUDIO SIGNALS

When audio is recorded via the recorder's internal tuner, or via the EIAJ 8-pin connector, the connections are the same as the video, and the signals are inputted automatically when the particular video input is selected.

If the line input is selected, audio will not record unless a separate audio input line is connected to the recorder. As in the case of connecting RF cables, the impedance/audio output must match that of the input to the recorder. All recorders have audio line level in-

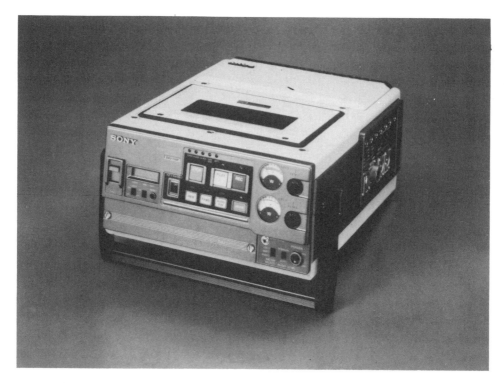

Figure 3.4: The Sony BVU-150 portable ³/₄-inch U-Matic SP incorporates the audio level control. Courtesy of the Sony Corporation.

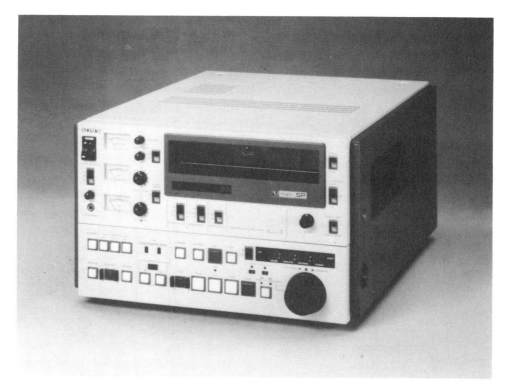

Figure 3.5: The Sony BVU-870 ³/₄-inch U-Matic SP recorder incorporates the audio limit and audio monitor switches. Courtesy of the Sony Corporation.

puts, while other, more featured recorders also have a line level input and a microphone level audio input. There are substantial differences in the impedances to each of these inputs. As such, they cannot be mixed.

A microphone cannot be plugged directly into the line input, and a line level device, such as the output from an audio tuner, cannot be plugged into the microphone input. If a recorder has only a line level input, a microphone can be used through an external amplifier or mixer which will change its output to line level.

Industrial recorders usually have more than one audio channel. Audio input signals can be used for either channel, provided the rules of matching signal impedances are followed. If the EIAJ 8-pin connector is used to input audio, the audio will be recorded on Channel 2. For this reason, Channel 2 is thought of as the main audio channel in multichannel recording.

Audio Level Control

In industrial recorders, the recording level is set with the audio level control. This control is used in conjunction with the audio level meter. The input level should be adjusted so the average of the level is set at 0 db. (See Figure 3.4.)

Audio Limiting

Sometimes during audio recording, the incoming signal peaks way over the 0 db point causing distortions in the recording. To prevent this, the operator can choose to limit these peaks by activating an audio limiting circuit. (See Figure 3.5.) When this circuit is on, distortions will be limited; however, the signal recorded on the tape will not be an exact reproduction of the incoming audio signal.

Audio Line Out

The audio line out from the recorder can be connected directly to the audio input of the monitor. When such connections are made, the output from the recorder and the input to the monitor must be at the same signal impedance level.

Incoming audio signals can be monitored either through an audio output line or through the 8-pin connector. Since this is a single line output, it is necessary to select the line input to be monitored, by using the audio monitor output channel switch, located on the recorder. The operator can select the input to Channel 1, Channel 2 or Mix, which monitors the output of both. (Refer to Figure 3.5.)

Mixing Audio Connectors

In some cases it might become necessary to mix balanced and unbalanced audio lines when connecting inputs and outputs. Just because audio signals are fed into the recorder via XLR connectors does not guarantee that the incoming signals are balanced. In order for an audio signal to be balanced, the output source, all connectors and wiring, and the recorder input must be balanced. If any point in this system is unbalanced, then the entire system will be unbalanced. Situations in which this occurs usually involve a balanced microphone that is hooked up to a recorder which can accept only an unbalanced input. Check the wiring of the microphone for proper connection to the recorder input.

INSERTING THE VIDEOCASSETTE

Inserting the videocassette into the recorder may seem easy. However, in the rush to either make a recording or play back a tape, it is possible to create a number of problems.

Videocassettes can only be inserted into the recorder in one way. The front end of the cassette contains a flap that will be opened by the recorder mechanism to expose the tape. The bottom side of the cassette contains the reel hubs that will be positioned over the supply and take-up reels to drive the tape. The top side of the cassette usually has a window which shows the amount of tape remaining on the supply and take-up reels. Insert the cassette with the front door flap away from you and the top tape window facing you. Inserting the tape cassette upside down can seriously damage the recorder transport mechanism. If the tape is new, it is a good idea to pack the tape. (For a discussion of tape packing, see Chapter 6 .) If the tape has been used, first check to see if the tape can be used for recording. Videotapes usually have lockouts which, when used, can prevent the accidental erasure of previously recorded material. On 1/2-inch cassettes this lockout is a plastic tab that is located on the opposite side of the front tape door flap. The lockout is activated when the tab is broken off. On 3/4-inch U-Matic cassettes, the record lockout is a red button located on the bottom of the cassette. Should you wish to record on tapes which have been record protected, simply place a small piece of tape over the lockout opening. (This will work for both 1/2-inch and 3/4-inch tapes. However, in the case of the latter it is strongly suggested that you re-use the red tab.) Next, observe the cassette tape window to see if the amount of tape remaining on the supply will be enough to meet your recording needs.

Videocassette Differences

There are a number of important differences between 1/2-inch and 3/4-inch videocassettes. First is their ability to reproduce still-frame pictures. All 1/2-inch videocassettes are capable of playing back a still frame. This is not the case with 3/4-inch U-Matic cassettes, where the cassette must be designed for still-frame playback. To determine whether or not a cassette is capable of still-frame playback, observe the cassette's underside where the reel hubs are located. A videocassette designed for still-frame playback has two small holes located near the red record lockout button. A cassette not designed for still-frame operation only has one.

The next difference is cassette size. Half-inch cassettes of the same format are all the same physical size. They differ only in the size of their center hubs, which determine the amount of tape they contain. Three-quarter inch cassettes come in two sizes: those used in full-sized recorders and those used in portables. The physical size of the latter is limited by the physical limitations of the portable cassette carriage. Its maximum recording time is only 20 minutes compared to a maximum recording time of 60 minutes for full-sized cassettes. When using a portable cassette in a standard 3/4-inch recorder, make sure the guide groove located on the underside of the videocassette is matched with the guide groove in the cassette carriage.

Front-Load Recorders

Many new 1/2-inch and 3/4-inch recorders use a front-loading mechanism. While the loading mechanism for top-loading recorders can either be electrical or mechanical, or a combination of both, front-loading recorders require that the power be on for tape loading and ejection. When loading a tape into this type of recorder, apply pressure to the point where the mechanism grabs the tape and completes the loading process. Never force the cassette. The same is true of the unloading process. Wait for the mechanism to complete the unloading process before removing the cassette.

RECORDER FUNCTIONS

Record Mode

After you have inserted the cassette into the recorder, make sure that all your connections are correct. Most consumer 1/2-inch recorders automatically go into the E to E mode when the power is turned on. For 3/4-inch recorders, press the record button to see the E to E signal and make sure the signal you want to record is displayed on the monitor. If it isn't, the input select switch is probably in the wrong position. Remember, in the case of recorders using an

Figure 3.6: Playback picture exhibiting streaking.

internal tuner, the output VCR/TV switch must be in the VCR position.

To activate the record mode, press PLAY and RECORD. Make sure the picture exhibited on the monitor in the E to E mode does not change. When the record mode is activated, recording is not instantaneous. The recorder transport mechanism requires approximately five to eight seconds to load the tape around the drum cylinder. Avoid giving the recorder any other instructions during this time. Let the recorder complete the instruction; otherwise, in the rush to respond to various recorder commands, the shuttling of the tape could cause it to throw a loop, which can result in tape damage. Three-quarter inch

recorders activate a stand-by lamp and lock out the entry of other commands.

Simple Front Panel Controls

Many of the front panel controls are self-explanatory and easy to operate. These functions are REWIND, FAST FORWARD, PLAY, STOP and EJECT. Many videotape recorders also have the ability to search at rapid speeds to find a particular point on the tape. These modes are sometimes referred to as REVIEW for reverse search and CUE for forward search. In order to enter these modes, place the recorder in the PLAY mode and select the desired direction of scan. To return to the PLAY mode, press the PLAY button.

Playback Mode

If playback appears to be noisy or exhibits streaking (see Figure 3.6), adjust the recorder's tracking control until the noise clears up. This control is used to electronically compensate for changes in the position of the control track pulse recorded on the tape. Tapes that are self-recorded (played back on the same unit they were recorded on) should have the best tracking. This means that during playback the tracking control should be in the FIXED position for best results. Tapes played back on different units will probably require some minor tracking control adjustment.

Some high-priced industrial recorders, particularly those used in editing systems, contain tracking meters, or meters that share duties with one of the audio channel inputs. If the recorder contains such a meter, it can be adjusted for maximum reading by turning the tracking control.

Skew Control

Like tape tracking, skew is a problem that results from the changing physical characteristics of the recorder and videotape. Recorder induced skew error is primarily dependent on the condition of the back tension band, and can be corrected by replacement of the band. Videotape induced skew error is caused by the exposure of the tape backing to varying thermal conditions. Unlike recorder induced error, it is not correctable with the videocassette.

Skew affects the synchronization of the horizontal and vertical signals. Any sync distortion introduced by skew error will affect editing and dubbing. In order to correct this condition, 3/4-inch recorders have a skew control. Cross pulse monitors delay the vertical and horizontal sync intervals so they are displayed in the active picture. Skew error begins at the head switching point, which is positioned directly

above, or in the vertical interval. Depending on the monitor used, the skew error might not even be visible on typically over scanned television monitors. This small amount of error can still cause problems in the editing or dubbing stages. The skew control can be used to minimize the amount of bending after the head switching point.

COMMON OPERATION PROBLEMS AND SOLUTIONS

Now that we have looked at simple videotape recorder operations let's take a look at some of the common problems you are likely to encounter. Most recorder problems are due to poor connections, user misunderstanding of recorder operations, or both.

The performance of videotape recorders containing internal tuners is dependent on the strength of the incoming antenna signal. In general, videotape recorders are far more sensitive to over-the-air distortions than the average television receiver. This is because recorders not only receive over-the-air signals, they also rely on the strength and position of sync signals for stable recording. (This condition is true for any input mode of signal to the recorder.)

Inputting the Over-The-Air Signal

Over-the-air signals received by the recorder are first processed into their baseband composite form. In order to do this, the signal received by the RF input of the recorder must be at least 175 microvolts for VHF or 200 microvolts for UHF. Baseband video signals must contain the standard video sync levels of 0.3 volts of sync and 0.3 volts of burst, along with their proper relationships for good color recordings. Weak signals often result in unstable playback.

Often, unstable playback is the result of loose or poorly wired connections at the input to the recorder. Good connections to the recorder's input not only require proper wiring, but also need the connector to be securely fastened to the video inputs. For this reason, avoid using plug converter adapters because they add resistance to the incoming signals and increase the possibility of loose connections.

No E to E Signal

If no E to E signal appears on your monitor, check input and output connections, and confirm that the recorder input selector is in the correct position. If the monitor has a multiple input selector, make sure its input selection switch is in the right position.

Snowy or Weak Output E to E Picture

If your recorder (recorders with internal tuners) has a snowy or weak output E to E picture, turn off the recorder tuner's automatic gain control and adjust the fine tuning for the best reception. Check to see that the recorder's RF modulator is set to the area's unused channel, and that the output receiver is set to the same channel. Select other channels on the record er's tuner and confirm that the problem is not just poor reception of one particular channel.

Color Input E to E Signal is
Black and White

Color and black-and-white mode selection is dependent on the signal amplitude and phase of the color burst signal. The videotape recorder samples the back porch of the horizontal line to confirm that these parameters are correct. If there are any problems in the burst signal, the recorder

will switch to black and white, rather than display a distorted color signal.

For recorders with internal tuners, check the fine tuning of both the recorder and the receiver's tuner. For industrial 3/4-inch recorders, confirm that the mode selection switch is in the automatic mode and not the black-and-white position.

Recorder Stops

All recorders contain a memory switch that places the recorder in the stop mode when the counter reaches all "zeros." This is a mechanical stop that has no relationship to any particular point on the tape. The memory counter is used to mark a particular position during record or playback. The recorder will stop if the counter is not reset.

During normal rewind, the memory counter should be set to "off" to prevent the recorder from going to the stop mode prior to reaching the beginning of tape.

Snowy Playback Picture

If your monitor displays a snowy picture, adjust the tracking control. If turning the tracking control does not clear up the picture, clean the video heads.

CONCLUSION

In this chapter we have looked at common videotape recorder operations. The following discussion in Chapter 4 will look at the operation of videotape recorders within editing systems.

4 Recorders Within Systems

Today, most video programming is shot "film style"—each scene is individually shot, often a number of times from different angles. Final decisions on programming content, therefore, have moved to the editing suite in which the tape recorder becomes part of an editing system.

In Chapter 3, we covered the record and playback functions of videotape recorders. In this chapter, we will look at the operations of VCRs within systems, and how they interface and react with other components.

COMPONENTS OF THE EDITING SYSTEM

The components of the editing system are divided into two primary areas—those that control the functions of the recorder over and above the functions that are available on the recorder, and those that provide external signal processing. The final video product we view usually has been recorded on a number of different recorders, pieced together on an editing system and processed through a time base corrector (TBC) and enhancer, among other equipment, to recover the quality that was lost during the editing and dubbing processes. Figure 4.1 illustrates a typical editing system.

Recorders

The editing system consists of a SOURCE machine, used to playback material, and an EDITOR (such as the JVC KR-M800U editing recorder or the JVC CR-850U professional editing recorder illustrated in Figures 4.2 and 4.3) that is used to record the individual segments. These machines must be far more precise than those used for ordinary playback—stability being the key factor in an editing system. First, the recorder must shuttle the tape to a point close to the selected edit mark. Next, the machines must go into their respective modes: PLAYBACK for the source machine and RECORD for the editor. The servo systems in the recorders must then drive the tape up to the proper speed for system reproduction. Finally, the recorder/editor must recognize the operator-selected edit point and piece the incoming video information together with the

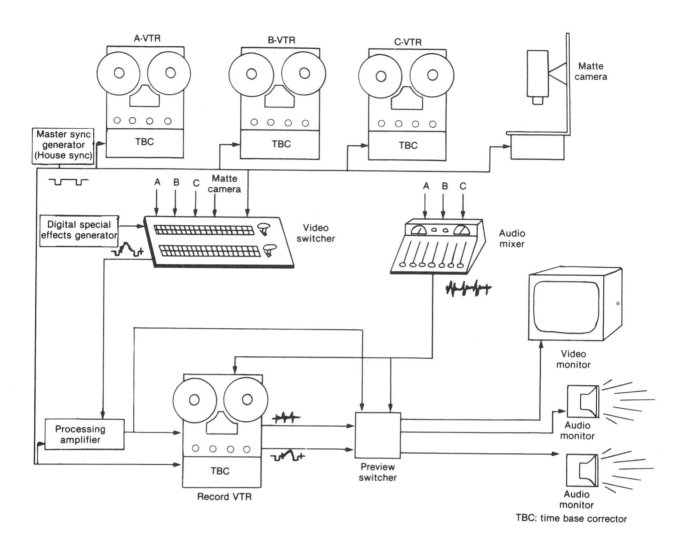

Figure 4.1: Typical editing system.

Source: Gary Anderson, *Video Editing and Post-Production, 2nd Edition*, Knowledge Industry Publications, Inc., 1988.

existing video information on the master tape. The capture of the video from the source by the editor has two requirements: The edit must occur close to the selected edit point and in the vertical interval. Individual scenes usually occur within a limited number of frames. If the edit occurs too far from the operator-selected point, the resulting composition of the edit could be far different from what the

operator intended. Multiple edits within a short period of time require a great deal of accuracy on the part of the editing unit.

The Edit Capture Point

Edits are usually timed to occur in the vertical interval so the transition between the master and source video occurs between the end

Figure 4.2: JVC CR-850U ³/₄-inch videocassette editing recorder. Courtesy JVC Company of America.

Figure 4.3: JVC KR-M800U MII editing recorder. Courtesy JVC Company of America.

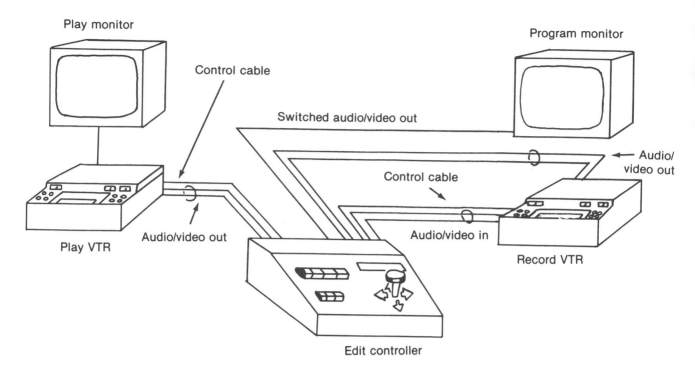

Figure 4.4: A two-VCR control-track editing system.

Source: Gary Anderson, *Video Editing and Post-Production, 2nd Edition*, Knowledge Industry Publications, Inc., 1988.

of one complete video frame and the beginning of the next. If the edit takes place in the active (viewable) video segment, the resulting distortion would make the edit useless. The edit capture point, therefore, must occur in a very limited space within the vertical interval. It cannot occur in the vertical sync, as the switch over between pictures would cause vertical sync distortion and a vertical roll at the edit point. The back porch blanking region is also restricted, since it contains the burst signal. Edits occurring at this point could cause a shift in color phase. This leaves only the front porch of vertical blanking. Placed on the front porch, the edit capture point represents approximately three horizontal lines.

Editing Recorder Mechanisms

Editing recorders have electronic and mechanical systems that are different from those of recorders used for general recording and playback. Editing recorders must have the ability to reference the playback signal to the incoming video signal from the source player. This requires that the recorder's capstan system (which is responsible for controlling tape speed) be operated by a separate servo control system. In addition, due to the accuracy required to move the tape to the proper edit point, the capstan shaft must be mounted directly to a drive motor to allow for changes in motor speed. This enables the incoming video from the source player to be coupled directly to the tape instead of channeled through a series of rubber drive belts. In a belt drive system, wear can lead to edit errors.

Tape transports must also be upgraded to handle the stress that results from shuttling the tape back and forth while searching for the edit point. Many high-end editing systems, and all of those that are advertised as professional or

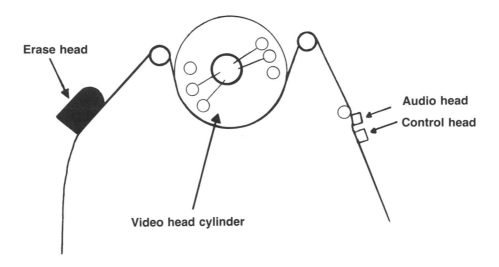

Figure 4.5: Placement of the erase, video and control heads on the tape path.

broadcast-quality, use two independent reel motors that are driven by individual servo motors. Like the capstan servo, (using direct-drive motors rather than rubber drive) direct-reel drive greatly increases shuttle accuracy.

Finally, both the source unit and editing recorder must be able to communicate with each other through a central controller that is used to select the edit points. This controller remotely commands both units. Figure 4.4 shows the position of the edit controller in a two-VCR control-track editing system.

TYPES OF EDITS

Editing is the process by which various sources of video are patched together on a single tape. Edits are defined by the number of signals on the tape that are replaced during the edit process, and fall into two general categories—assembly edits and insert edits. When all information on the edit master tape is replaced during editing, the edit is called an assembly edit. When just the video signal is replaced, the edit is called an insert edit.

Assembly Edits

During the assembly edit process, the recorder goes into the full record mode and the full erase head is energized. The video, audio and control track heads then record the new signals on the master tape.

Figure 4.5 shows that the erase, video and control heads are separated by a physical space. This spacing equates to precise timing requirements in the assembly edit process. The process of saturating the various heads for recording, however, is not linear. The timing of all editing processes is determined by the electronics of the assembly edit circuits, which are timed to take into account these physical separations. As the electronic circuit timing can never exactly match that of the physical difference, the quality of the transition between video sources can be affected. When the recorder receives the command to go into the edit mode, the full erase head will begin to erase the previously recorded video. There is, however, a section of tape that exists between the full erase head and the video heads that is

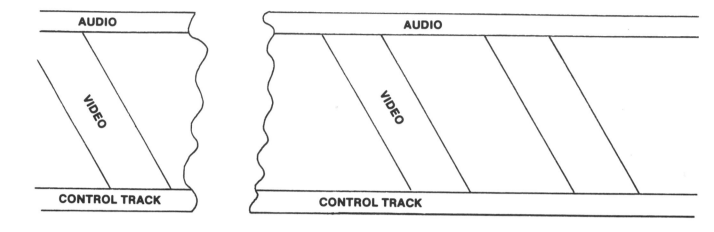

Figure 4.6: Tape with jagged edges after assembly edit.

not subject to erasure by the full erase head. This section of tape is directly recorded over by the new signal that is applied to the video heads. As the record current applied to the video heads is much weaker than the signal applied to the tape by the full erase head, the transition point between edits can be subject to noisy distortions. To overcome this problem, a process called "backspace editing" is employed.

Backspace Editing

During backspace editing, the tape is moved back a number of frames prior to the start of the selected edit point. This allows time for the recorder's transports and servo system to come up to their proper recording speeds. While this process allows the playback video to lock into the incoming video, it has little effect on the actual edit start point. As a result, valuable frames of video information can be lost as the new information is placed over the old.

Edit Start and Stop Points

Selecting an edit start point that is too close to the edit stop point of the source video can also have its disadvantages. Tape slippage can cause frames of unrecorded tape to appear between the end of the existing information on the tape and the start of the new information. Many an editor has been frustrated by attempts to properly position the start point of an assembly edit.

Servo Error

Loss of video information isn't the only potential problem of assembly edits—the loss of control track pulses can cause the recorder's servos to unlock during playback. The distortion that occurs during the four-to-seven-second period while the recorder relocks can make an edit useless. Even small differences in timing can create problems. At the edit start point, the difference in control track timing can result

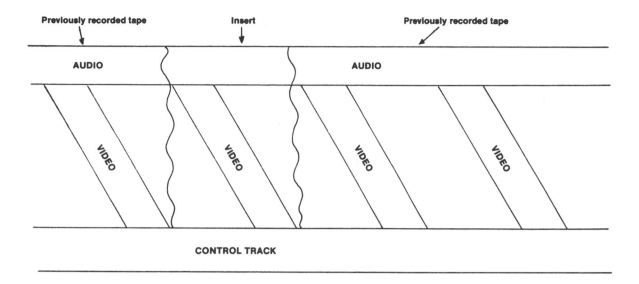

Figure 4.7: Videotape with insert edit.

in the need for the recorder's servo to readjust itself. The increased servo error that results may not be apparent during the original edit. After dubbing the tape, however, jitter is created that can go beyond the servo handling capability of the recorder's servo system. Second generation dubs from these edited masters can cause the monitor to roll at the edit point.

Jagged-Edge Output

At the edit stop point of an assembly edit there is no relationship to the video that follows—it is the same as pushing the stop button during recording. The jagged-edge output that results is uneven and difficult to match up with other tape. (See Figure 4.6.)This is the major drawback of the assembly edit process: the inability to insert video between two sections of recorded video.

Insert Edits

The need to insert video segments between existing video on the master tape led to the development of the "insert" editing system. Insert edits replace or insert individual segments of video between existing sections of video. To avoid the problems involved in maintaining synchronization that make short inserts impossible during assembly edits, insert edit systems replace only the video information, while maintaining the previously recorded control track. (See Figure 4.7.)

By maintaining a constant control track, a constant and stable reference signal is established for the recorder. This means that once the editor/recorder references itself to the incoming video from the source playback unit, no further realignment of the servos is required at the edit point.   By doing this, however, the full erase head cannot be activated to ensure that the video heads will be applying new signals to a basically blank tape. (Remember, the strength of the signal applied to the video head is not strong enough to completely override the existing video signal.) In addition, the recorder's servo system must be extremely accurate if the video head is to be placed in an exact relationship to the previously recorded video. Even if this is accomplished, we are still faced with a problem similar to that found in assembly editing. The weakness of the record current does not allow for a clean transition between the old and new video. Some recorders compensate for this by increasing the strength of the record current at the edit-in point of the insert process. This process, known as "over-recording," uses the strength of the new recording signal to record over the old one, and usually causes color streaking or a rainbow effect during the first few seconds of the edit. The edit-out point also has problems for similar reasons. The record current applied to the video head cannot just stop at the edit-out point. Residue magnetism remains with the head, which can cause video distortion.

Flying Erase Heads

To compensate for this problem, advanced editing systems mount a set of erase heads in the head cylinder before and at a slight angle to the video heads. These heads, known as flying erase heads, can be turned on at the edit-in point and turned off at the edit-out point. The lower the amount of record current applied to the video heads, the less time it will take to saturate the heads at the edit-in point and desaturate the heads at the edit-out point. By recording over an erased track with a head that quickly accepts a new signal an extremely accurate edit can be achieved. Since there is no change in the control track that provides stability, editing in the insert mode with flying erase heads is the most preferred form of professional editing.

PREPARING THE TAPE FOR EDITING

Since the editing process requires that signals be taken from and applied to videotape, the condition of the tape plays a vital role in the editing process. All the conditions that apply to good recording also apply to good editing. Make sure the tapes you use are of good quality and that prior to making any recordings the tapes are properly packed. (See Chapter 6 for a discussion of tape packing.) Keep in mind that a key factor in editing is the recording of a stable control track. Errors in video can be corrected to some degree through the use of external processing equipment; however, the loss of a properly recorded control track can cause the source recorder's servo to unlock making editing impossible. The time required to relock a servo system can be as great as five seconds—in terms of edit time, this can mean the loss of an important part of a production.

PREPARING THE PROGRAM

Since most video productions eventually end up in the editing suite, each segment of recorded video must be planned and shot with its place in the editing and post-production process in mind. When you record source material, you should never begin or end the recording with the actual amount of material you plan to edit. The usable material must be buffered at both the beginning and the end.

The recorded material prior to the segment you wish to edit is used to lock up the source unit's servo system and to provide a stable reference for the editor servos. If the phase of the editor's playback video is not matched to that coming from the source unit, a clean edit is not possible. Most editing systems preroll the tape approximately five seconds prior to the edit-in point, so the introduction recording time before the usable video must, at least, match that amount of time. "At least" does not allow room for error. As a general rule, the recorded lead-in time should be approximately 15 to 20 seconds.

Stability considerations at the edit-out point are just as important as they are at the edit-in point. It is difficult to make editing decisions during a shoot and have them work out perfectly during post-production. Calling for a stop tape at the end of a scene can cause the recorder to lose valuable information as the tape is jerked away from the video heads. In order to provide latitude for selection of the edit-out point, it is again best to allow between 15 and 20 seconds of recording time after a scene is shot.

BLACK BURST

If we assume that a program will be pieced together in the insert mode, we can prepare the master tape that will be used on the editing recorder by separating the synchronization control track pulses from the video information. By doing so, we can use "black burst" to create a stable control track pulse over the duration of the tape. Black burst is a video signal that contains all the necessary sync elements of the television signal. Black burst contains horizontal and vertical sync and blanking, along with the color burst signal. Due to the comprehensive nature of the signal it is used as a standard synchronization signal for mixing signals from various video sources. For editing purposes the use of black burst has two advantages. First, constant sync yields constant control track pulses, which result in stable servo operation. Second, black burst appears on a television monitor as a black picture. When black is used as a foundation, spaces between edits are less noticeable than either snow or other active video signals.

Generating Black Burst

A tape can be black bursted at any time. The process is as easy as inputting a signal into the recorder and coming back an hour later

to change tapes. Since source tapes require the recording of completely new information, it is of no use to black burst tapes used for source recording. The process is therefore reserved for master edit tapes.

Black burst is generally available as an output from most sync generators. Since a sync generator is not a mandatory requirement for an editing system, it is possible that some editing system operators will not have one. If this is the case, there are a number of options. Sync generators can be rented or tapes can be sent out for black bursting. Due to the expense of both solutions, they are only practical if a large number of tapes require black bursting. If this is not the case, black burst can be obtained from most color cameras. Just close down the camera iris or cap the camera lens and the resulting signal output is black burst. This method does have a number of minor trade-offs, however. First, any time the camera is on, the pickup tube is using up some of its operating life. Second, the quality of the visible black signal generated by the camera is dependent on the quality of the image pickup tubes, where it can be somewhat noisier than the black generated by a sync generator.

TIME CODE

The use of time code in your system will be determined by a number of factors. First, and most important, does the edit controller you use recognize time code? All edit controllers use control track pulses to recognize the edit point, but only those controllers specified to recognize time code can utilize the signal. If you are uncertain about the controller in your system, check the manufacturer's specification sheet or look for a time code input on the controller. The signal is usually inputted to the controller via an RCA connector.

If you use a time code edit controller you are not limited to editing with time code tapes. Many previously recorded tapes, particularly those recorded on portable decks, do not have time code. These tapes can be used by placing the time code/control track switch, located on the controller, in the control track position. Even if you forget to flip the switch, most controllers will automatically read the control track pulses when time code is not available. This capability also helps to maintain editing accuracy during slow tape speeds when the time code signal amplitude is too low to read.

Can Your Recorder Read Time Code?

As previously noted, not all recorders are capable of reading time code. As in the case of the controller, if you are uncertain about your recorder, check the time code input and output (usually RCA connectors). Attempting to record and read time code through the standard audio circuits can lead to inaccurate edits on the part of the controller.

Inability of your recorder to use longitudinal time code still leaves the possibility of using vertical interval time code. (Time code can also be recorded by the video heads on a portion of the video tracks.) Although vertical interval time code systems are more expensive than equipment used to generate and read longitudinal time code, the cost of the overall system is less than it would be to replace a recorder.

When purchasing time code equipment, remember that the generating system must be matched by the reader. A longitudinal recording cannot be read by a vertical interval reader and vice versa. A longitudinal time code recording is one in which the time code is recorded on a separate track. Readers incorporated in edit controllers usually read only longitudinal code. In order for these to operate with vertical interval time code (VITC), the video signal must first be passed through the VITC reader and then sent to the controller. Figure 4.8 illustrates the difference between vertical interval and longitudinal time code recording.

SIGNAL PROCESSING

The electro-mechanical transport system of the videotape recorder that can cause editing inaccuracies is also responsible for introducing video problems into the playback signal.

The stability of the playback signal is dependent upon the stability of the tape transport. In helical recording systems, each of two video heads is responsible for producing one video field. This, in turn, requires that the tape be wrapped around the scanner that contains the video heads. The length of the track can lead to tension errors as the tape is pulled around the video head drum assembly. Distortion most often occurs at the beginning of the video field when the moving tape first makes contact with the spinning drum assembly; a condition known as entrance shock.

Transport errors are further compounded by the rest of the transport system, particularly the capstan pinch roller. This component is responsible for pulling the tape evenly and loading it onto the take-up reel. The timing of the playback video sync signal is dependent upon the consistency of the recorder's transport. As a result, a mechanical device can never reproduce signals with the same stability as a purely electronic device.

Instability caused by a recorder's transport results in a playback vertical sync that jitters in relationship to the stable vertical sync generated from a camera. This movement of sync from the playback video is known as a recorder's "jitter factor." Because jitter factor is dependent upon the recorder's mechanics, rubber drive transports have a greater jitter factor than direct-drive motor recorders.

Jitter and Its Effects on Tape Playback

Color

For vertical sync, which has a long duration, the effects of playback jitter are not noticeable on the playback tape. Color signals, which occur over a shorter duration, are another matter. In order for the tape to playback with a constant hue, the color signal must have a great deal of stability. Under normal playback conditions jitter could cause the hue of a picture to change to such a degree that the playback picture would

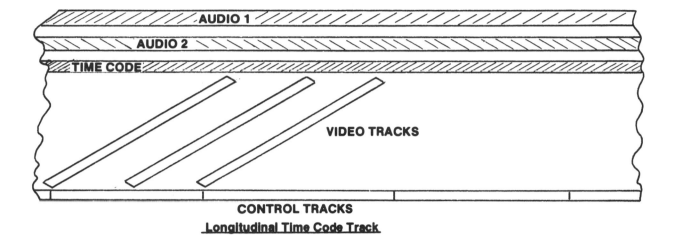

CONTROL TRACKS

Longitudinal Time Code Track

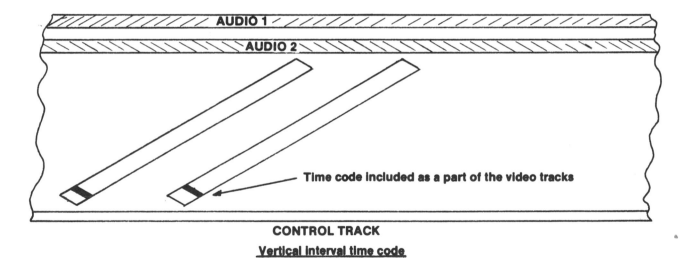

CONTROL TRACK

Vertical interval time code

Figure 4.8: Longitudinal time code vs. vertical interval time code as recorded on tape.

be unusable. To prevent this, color jitter is internally processed by the recorder. The circuits used are the automatic frequency control (AFC) and the automatic phase control (APC). The result is increased stability, enough to maintain a viewable color playback picture.

Multiple Generations

With each new tape generation, tape jitter can double. Once again, the effects of vertical sync jitter are not noticeable on the playback monitor, but the shorter duration color signal quickly falls out of the control range of the AFC/APC circuits. As a result, a third generation tape can exhibit distorted color.

Editing also places great demands on the playback tape as the stability of both the source and editing units depend on the stability of the playback tape. Jitter in the playback tape can cause inaccuracy in the edit. If a production requires three or four generations, the final product can be fairly unstable.

Time Base Correctors

Time base correctors are designed to replace the stability lost by recorders' mechanical systems. They compare the sync and color jitter from the tape to a stable sync and color reference.

Time base correctors can do little to restore signal resolution or signal-to-noise ratio lost in copying tape, but they present a stable sync source to the editor. Editing systems that use a time base corrector's reference to a stable sync source obtain more accurate edits with less distortion at the edit point. Multiple generations of tapes processed through a time base corrector exhibit less of the sync and color distortion found in systems that do not include a TBC.

Time Base Correctors and System Integration

The source sync that provides the reference for the time base corrector can be generated internally or taken from another stable source such as a sync generator. When a time base corrector is configured to accept an external

sync source it can be used to integrate a playback tape as a video source in a production system. The tape can be mixed via a switcher as a source for special effects or titles.

Selecting the Time Base Corrector

Selection of a time base corrector is a process that requires matching needs with the recorder. If you already own a videotape recorder, it will be necessary to determine the amount of jitter in the playback signal. The operating range of a time base corrector is expressed in terms of the amount of horizontal lines of jitter it can correct. This is known as the time base corrector's ''window of correction.'' For the time base corrector to be effective, its window must be greater than a recorder's horizontal jitter. Non-capstan servo recorders exhibit the greatest amount of horizontal jitter and should be matched to time base correctors with at least 16 horizontal lines of correction. Direct-drive capstan servo recorders produce the least, and can be used with time base correctors with as low as two lines of correction.

When considering the amount of correction required, remember that not all tapes will be played back on the same unit they were recorded on. When tapes are played back on a different recorder, the amount of transport jitter increases due to the physical differences between the two recorders. Additional jitter can also be present due to physical changes in tapes, such as tape stretch. The biggest jitter ''bugs'' come from shooting video on portable recorders. Field production is usually done with the recorder in every position except the one that is best for the recorder—laying flat on the ground. Any movement of the recorder, during recording, can cause a gyroscopic effect that unlocks the servo system and results in unusable video. Horizontal errors caused by this gyroscopic effect can be beyond the range of any time base corrector.

CONCLUSION

In this chapter, we looked at the operations of videotape recorders within editing systems. In Chapter 5, we will discuss videotape recording and playback processes.

5 Videotape Recorders: Record and Playback Processes

In Chapters 3 and 4, we touched on the operation of videotape recorders. In this chapter, we will discuss recorder record and playback processes.

The ability of a recorder to perform is keyed to its recording and playback processes. These consist of three major requirements:

1. The recorder must be able to playback its own recorded signal.
2. The playback signal must conform to the television standards of the playback monitor.
3. The signal recorded on tape by one recorder must be able to be played back on any other recorder of the same format.

Regardless of its format, a recorder's electronic function is to place a signal on the tape during recording, and recover it during playback.

Although the same principles that apply to audio recording also apply to video, it is the degree of accuracy required that separates the two. Small changes in audiotape speed—wow and flutter—are not detected until they vary

greatly from the constant tape speed. Minor changes are usually a result of a loss of frequency response. For videotape recorders the same minor changes can result in totally unusable pictures. The phase and pulse widths of the playback picture sync are dependent upon the consistency of both the tape and head speeds. Since the mechanisms responsible for tape transport in a recorder rely on rubber components, they are more vulnerable to breakdown than the electronic components. In order to understand the need for accuracy it is first necessary to understand how signals are written on and read off of the tape.

THE TAPE PATH

During the recording process the tape is pulled across a rotating upper drum cylinder that contains the video heads. Regardless of the total number of video heads, only two are used during recording; each records one video field of 262.5 horizontal lines. During a single rotation of the upper drum cylinder, a complete frame of video is recorded. In order for the

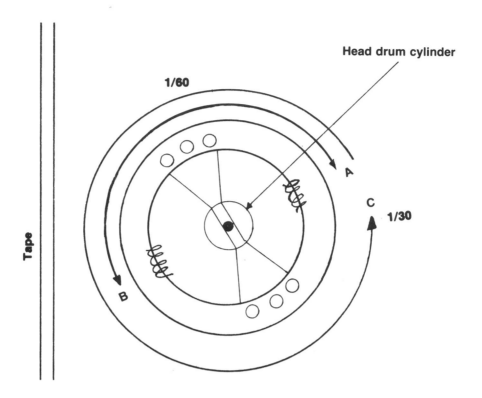

Figure 5.1: The head cylinder makes 1800 revolutions per minute.

recorder to reproduce an NTSC signal, the amount of time between contacts of each video head and the tape must be 1/60th of a second—it takes 1/30th of a second to complete 1800 head cylinder revolutions per minute (see Figure 5.1). This method of recording and playback corresponds to the television scanning process. Each pass of the video head must occur at the same time the monitor beam is scanning one television field. As the monitor beam blanks out and returns to the top of the screen to start the next field, one video head is beginning its contact with the tape, while the other is at its last contact point. In order to accommodate the time it takes for one video head to record one field of video, the videotape must be wrapped around the head cylinder 1 1/2 times the cylinder's circumference. This physical relationship between the moving video heads and the tape causes the video track to be recorded at an angle less than 90% to

the tape. Recorders employing this tape angle are referred to as a slant track recorders (STR).

THE GUARD BAND

Just as each field in the television scanning process can be thought of as an individual picture, so can the signal recorded by each pass of a video head. During the television scanning process, each field is separated by the vertical blanking interval. No such separation exists for the recorded fields on the videotape, since the blanking interval is recorded as part of the video track. Lack of video track separation can create a number of problems. If the tape did not move, each video head would keep recording one video track, one over the other; the result would be unusable. Even moving the tape so that the tracks are recorded adjacent to each other will not solve the problem. Magnetic flux lines from the video head are not limited

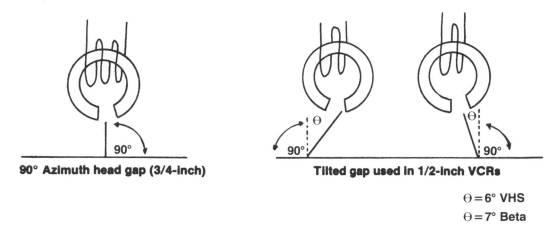

90° Azimuth head gap (3/4-inch)   Tilted gap used in 1/2-inch VCRs

$\Theta = 6°$ VHS
$\Theta = 7°$ Beta

Figure 5.2: Head gap azimuth angles.

by the physical width of the video head. As such, the flux lines spill over, covering an area greater than the head width. If the tracks were laid down next to each other, the spillover from the signal recorded from one head would degrade the signal recorded by the other. In order to prevent track to track interference, each track must be separated by a physical space on the tape. This space is called the guard band. During recording, the video tracks must be evenly laid down and separated by evenly spaced guard bands. This spacing is a function of the video heads mounted 180° apart on the upper drum cylinder, and a consistent tape speed. During playback, the video head expects to read the information at the same rate as it was written during the recording process. Any deviation of the video head reading along the video track will cause noise in the output picture. This noise is usually referred to as tracking noise.

HEAD AZIMUTH: DETERMINING THE TYPE OF GUARD BAND

3/4-inch U-Matic

Of all the tape formats currently available, the 3/4-inch U-Matic format remains as the primary standard of industrial grade recording. This recording format uses two video heads, each with the same azimuth. Azimuth refers to the angle of video head, when the gap is viewed straight on. For the U-Matic format, the head azimuth is perpendicular to the travel of the videotape (see Figure 5.2). Similar head azimuths record signals on tape at the same angle even though each track contains different information. As a result, each head can read the signal recorded by the other. Any crossover of information from one track to the other will degrade the overall output picture. For this reason, the tape speed of the U-Matic recorder had to take into account the width of the video head (approximately 100 microns), as well as the guard band between the tracks (approximately 59 microns). The amount of tape real estate required for both video track and guard band (159 microns) limits the total recording time of 3/4-inch tape to one hour.

1/2-inch

The longer recording times of the 1/2-inch tape formats were achieved by a reduction in tape speed. This reduction in speed crowded the video tracks together and physically eliminated the guard band. To prevent crosstalk be-

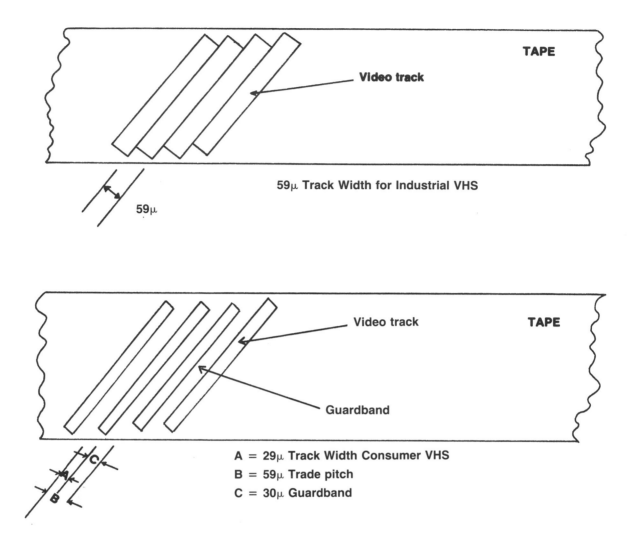

Figure 5.3: Comparison of VHS industrial and consumer formats.

tween the video tracks, the head azimuth was changed. By offsetting the video head gaps in equal and opposite directions, the signals recorded by one video head and played back by another would be reduced to near zero (see Figure 5.2). The system of azimuth recording found in Beta and VHS recorders ensures that one video head will not pick up any interference or crosstalk from adjacent tracks. In effect, the adjacent video track becomes the guard band for the preceeding and following video tracks. For VHS, the head azimuth is +/− 6° to the perpendicular; for Beta, the azimuth is +/− 7°.

Industrial 1/2-inch recorders that record at the fastest speeds, achieve the best picture reproduction through a combination of this high tape speed and wide video heads. Half-inch recorders that employ longer recording times compress the tracks further and require smaller video head widths. Multiple speed consumer recorders with two heads use both guard band and azimuth recording. For example, let's look at the VHS system. In the two-hour mode, the

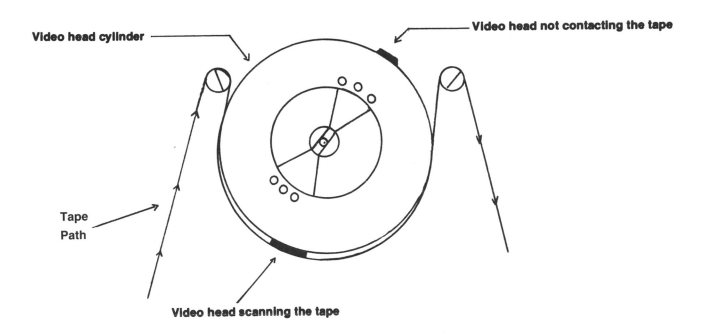

Video head cylinder

Video head not contacting the tape

Tape
Path

Video head scanning the tape

Figure 5.4: During playback, the head NOT scanning the tape should be switched off.

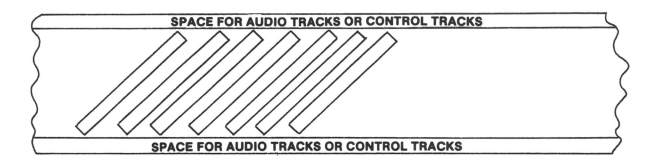

SPACE FOR AUDIO TRACKS OR CONTROL TRACKS

SPACE FOR AUDIO TRACKS OR CONTROL TRACKS

Figure 5.5: There is room on the videotape for more than just the video tracks.

tape speed of 33.3 mm/sec creates an effective track width of 59 microns. For the industrial version of VHS this also represents the width of the video head. Recorders with two heads that record for two, four and six hours use a video head width of just 29 microns (see Figure 5.3). The two-hour mode creates a physical guard band of 30 microns, while the six-hour mode relies on azimuth recording to avoid crosstalk.

TAPE SPEED: THE CONTROL TRACK PULSE

After the video tracks are written, the tape passes to the control track head where control pulses are recorded on the tape. Because of the 180° physical positioning of the heads, a control track pulse is required for only every other recorded field. For this reason control track pulses are recorded at a 30-Hz rate (one for every two video tracks). The control track pulse is positioned during recording at the point where one video head first makes contact with the tape. Provided that the head cylinder speed remains constant, the other head will write the next video field at the correct time. During playback, small variations in tape speed due to differences in tape transports and tape stretch can be corrected by adjusting the recorder's tracking control.

During recording, the signal is applied to the video heads at all times. During playback, however, each video head can only be active when it is in contact with the tape. If both heads were active at all times during playback, the video head not in contact with the tape would produce noise and degrade the output picture (see Figure 5.4.) To prevent this condition, the head amplifiers of each head are switched on and off during playback at the point where both video heads are making contact with the tape.

THE AUDIO TRACK

Audio signals are recorded on videotape in the same manner that they are recorded on conventional audiotape. Signals are transferred to the tape by a stationary head that records on a linear track. Recorders can have one, two or three audio tracks. The number of audio tracks is a function of the type of recorder. Industrial recorders usually use the second and third channels for stereo and time code information.

The audio and control tracks can be positioned either on the top or bottom edge of the tape, depending on the format (see Figure 5.5). The actual positioning of these signals is not as important as recognizing them in order to correctly align the control track and audio heads, especially during the post-production process.

PUTTING SIGNALS ON TAPE

Recording the Video Signal

In Chapter 1, we identified the various components that make up the video signal. These are:

1. Video—the luminance value that provides details.
2. Burst/Chroma—the color information.
3. Sync—the information that provides the timing reference.

With the exception of the sync and burst information, the actual visual video signal does not contain any regular or repeating information. The images that create the video signal vary not only within the recorded scene, but also from scene to scene. This in turn results in varying signal output voltages. The dark scene sections result in low output voltages, while the bright scene areas yield high output voltages. The video signal cannot be recorded on tape in this form. In order to transfer signals from the video head onto the tape, the video signal must be represented by a high-frequency sine wave. (See Figure 5.6.) This process is known as instantaneous modulation. It occurs by letting the video signal control the instantaneous frequency of the sine wave. The fre-

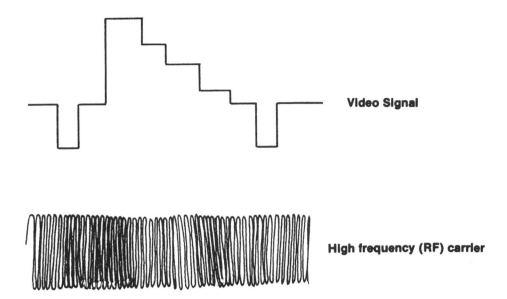

Figure 5.6: The video signal will be modulated by a carrier wave whose resting frequency is about twice that of the highest video frequency.

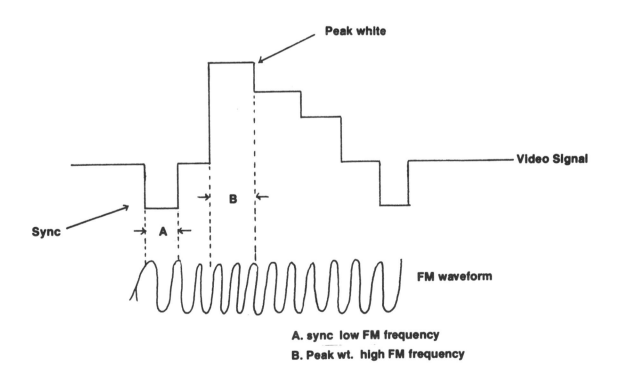

A. sync low FM frequency

B. Peak wt. high FM frequency

Figure 5.7: The highest levels of the video signal cause the modulator to run at its highest frequency.

quency will vary in proportion to the signal voltage level. The lowest voltage signal level, the sync signal, yields the lowest frequency. The highest signal levels, those representing the brightest portions of the video signal, result in the highest frequencies (see Figure 5.7). Since the *rate* of the sine wave (not the amplitude) varies, the process is called frequency modulation (FM).

In order for the modulator to produce an FM signal that is a true representation of the incoming video, the modulator must swing between the lowest and highest frequencies during each horizontal line of video. Because scene illumination does not always yield a full video signal (0.7 volts), forcing the video to a high level to meet the requirements of the modulator would distort the fidelity of the output signal. To prevent this, the modulator is preceeded by an automatic gain control circuit (AGC). This circuit inserts a 0.7 volt signal pulse (key) on the back porch of each horizontal line, outside of the active video. The use of a keyed AGC signal satisfies the need to swing the modulator over its complete range, while insuring that the signal recorded on the tape is a true representation of the incoming signal.

As noted in Chapter 2, the differences in the signals applied to tape generally fall into two categories: the direct record method and the converted subcarrier method. For the direct record method (usually used for broadcast recorders), the modulator allows the complete bandwidth of the video signal to be unchanged during processing. The modulator processes signals ranging from the 60-Hz sync signal to 4.2 MHz which represents the brightest portion of the video signal. Industrial grade recorders lack the frequency response of broadcast recorders because of their writing speeds, which require that the video signal be modulated into a narrower FM bandwidth. While the exact bandwidth differs from format to format, in all cases the 3.58-MHz subcarrier will be modulated separately into a frequency lower than that of the lowest video FM frequency.

The FM signal is continuously applied to the video heads during the recording process. The drive system is responsible for positioning the head so that the start of the field will coincide with the initial contact point of the video head.

RECORDING THE AUDIO SIGNAL

The principles and circuitry that are used in standard audio recording are used to record audio signals on videotape. And, as with video frequencies, the speed of the tape will determine the overall frequency response and therefore the overall quality of the recorded audio signal. Audio signals are very low in frequency compared to video signals, and as such there is no need to route the signal through a conversion process. This makes audio recording a simple process.

Audio signals are amplified and controlled by an AGC circuit, and fed to the audio head. The only additional processing consists of applying a bias signal to produce a more linear recording.

THE RECORDER'S SERVO SYSTEM

Speed Control

The recorder's servo system is designed to control the speed of the rotating video head cylinder and the speed of the videotape. The speed of the video head cylinder in the record mode is designed to allow the video tracks to be recorded at the NTSC rate of 30 frames (60 fields) per second. The speed of the tape must guarantee that the video tracks will be evenly spaced and separated by equal guard bands. Within the recorder, the speeds of the tape and head motors are not independent, but must interact in order to maintain the necessary phase relationships of signals on the tape.

A servo system is designed to compare two references, one fixed and the other variable. The function of a servo is to automatically adjust the variable reference to be like that of the fixed reference. Servo circuits consist of two parts—speed and phase. The speed section is responsible for providing the main drive power to the motor. The phase section represents the major servo action. It is responsible for either slightly speeding up or slightly slowing down the motor so that the phase of the video tracks matches that of the fixed reference.

The physics of any motor drive system makes it easier to slow down than to speed up. Therefore, in the VCR, the uncontrolled or "freerun" speed of the motor is always kept slightly above the desired speed. In order to control the speed of the motor, the servo system acts like a brake, slowing down the motor, and then releasing it to speed it up.

In the record mode the VCR takes its reference from the incoming video signal's vertical sync, which is separated from the video signal and wave shaped into a 30-Hz signal. Since the vertical sync signal is a stable signal, it is used as the fixed reference. For the head cylinder the variable reference is generated by small magnets located on the stationary lower cylinder. As the upper portion of the cylinder (the section containing the video heads) rotates, the magnetic fields are cut, producing a pulse (one negative and one positive) during each head rotation. This is referred to as the cylinder pulse generator (PG). This pulse is then wave shaped and keyed to the vertical sync reference pulse. The process is known as ramp and sample or sample and hold, and occurs because one of the reference signals is shaped into a form having a ramp (usually a trapezoidal waveform) and the other pulse is shaped into a spike that samples the voltage of the ramp. The resulting output voltage comes from the positioning of the spike on the ramp. To better understand this concept, we will assume that vertical sync is the source for the trapezoidal wave and that the spike pulse is created from the cylinder PG. Which waveform is created from which source signal is a function of the design of the servo system. Regardless, the theory behind servo operation remains the same. Since the trapezoidal waveform signal

comes from the vertical sync, it will act as our fixed reference in this discussion. (See Figures 5.8 and 5.9)

The spike pulse from the cylinder PG will vary in time due to the small instabilities of the motor. As a result, so will the timing of the pulse. For example, if the speed of the motor is too slow the PG frequency will decrease, and the spike will ride higher on the ramp, generating a higher than normal sample and hold voltage. If the motor speed is too fast, the pulse PG will occur at a faster rate, ride lower on the ramp, and in turn generate a lower than normal sample and hold voltage. In our example, the higher sample and hold voltage would have the effect of speeding up the motor, while the lower voltage would have the effect of slowing it down.

Phase Reference

Speed control is only one function of the servo—phase is the other. The various reference signals are wave shaped so that the sampling will occur at the point when one video head is making its initial contact with the tape and the other is finishing its contact. This assures that one video head is in contact with the tape during the complete duration of a video field. As we discussed earlier, the video heads' signals must alternately be switched on and off during playback so that unwanted noise can be eliminated. This head switching action, however, causes distortion right at the point of the switch. It should occur as close to the vertical blanking interval as possible. Since playback speed and phase must match that of the record mode, the head switching point relationship to the vertical blanking is determined by the record servo.

Tape Speed (Capstan) Servo

The capstan servo operates along the same principles as the cylinder servo. The vertical sync acts as the fixed reference, and the variable reference is taken from a frequency generator located

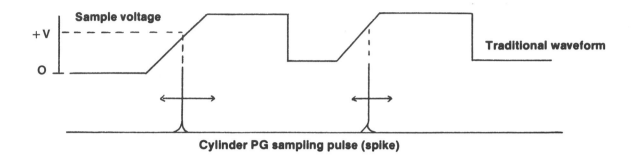

Figure 5.8: The PG sampling pulse can vary in its timing, so that the voltage it samples will likewise vary.

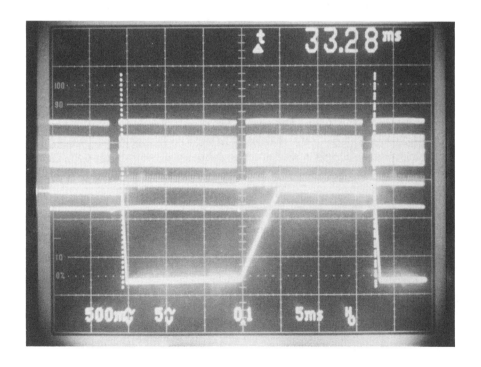

Figure 5.9: Incoming trapezoidal waveform as viewed on a waveform monitor.

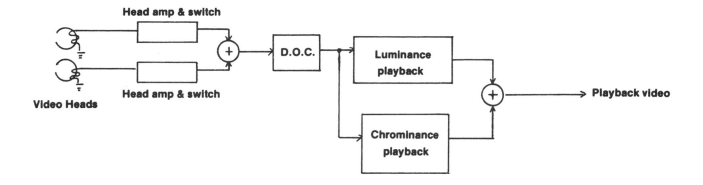

Figure 5.10: Block diagram of playback signal path.

on the bottom of the capstan motor. The operation of the sample and hold remains the same. During recording, the capstan servo electronically sets the reference for playback tape speed in much the same way that the cylinder servo positions the video heads. In addition to the vertical sync serving as the fixed reference for both the cylinder and capstan record servos, it is divided in half, shaped into a spike pulse and used as the control track signal. The actual recording of the control track on tape has no affect on the operation of the recording servo system. However, the operation of the capstan playback servo is dependent on the presence of this pulse.

THE PLAYBACK PROCESS

Playing Back Video

During playback, the playback amplifier for each head is turned on by the servo system only when the video head is in contact with the tape. (Figure 5.10 illustrates the signal path of playback video.) The output from each video head is mixed at a 30-Hz rate and combined to resemble the record FM signal. The signal

is then passed through a Dropout Compensation Circuit (DOC), which is designed to make up for playback signal losses. This loss occurs during playback when contact is lost between the video head and tape, or when the tape lacks oxide and is unable to record the FM. These losses, which are referred to as "dropout," normally appear as spotted noise in the output signal. The DOC circuit detects these losses and replaces the dropout with the last good line of video information. Because the eye tends to integrate video information within the frame, the repetition of an individual horizontal line of video is less noticeable than dropout noise. After the signal passes through the DOC circuit, it moves to the FM Demodulator where it is transformed back into a composite video signal.

While playback luminance signal processing is fairly straight forward, color processing is not. The FM signal recovered from the video heads is subject to jitter because of the mechanics of the tape transport, capstan and cylinder motors. This jitter has little affect on the luminance signal and is only dependent on reproducing the horizontal and vertical sync

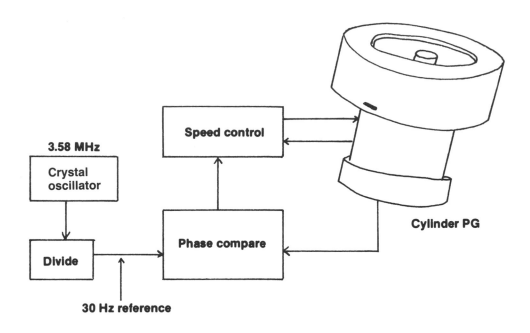

Figure 5.11: Basic cylinder servo diagram of playback signal path.

signals. Television sets are designed to overlook minor timing problems in these areas. The reproduction of color signals, however, requires that the phase of the 3.58-MHz signal vary no more than 2.6%. Variations greater than this will cause the playback monitor or television set to switch to black and white, rather than display a distorted signal. To prevent this, the converted subcarrier signal is balance modulated with a signal having an equal jitter factor. A Balance Modulator is a circuit that mixes two frequencies and outputs both the sum and the difference of the two input frequencies. Since the difference between these two output frequencies is great, either can be selected by passing the output through a high pass filter, in the case of the sum, or a low pass filter, in the case of the difference between the two. In 3/4-inch U-Matic recorders, the converted subcarrier fre-

quency recorded on tape is 688 kHz. To recover a stable 3.58-MHz color subcarrier in playback, the subcarrier is balance modulated with a 4.27 MHz + 4.96 MHz + 2 times jitter frequency (sum). The accurate cancellation of the jitter frequency is dependent upon the accuracy of the 4.27-MHz signal. This signal is created by a combination of the Automatic Phase Control (APC) and Automatic Frequency Control (AFC).

Playback Audio

The playback of audio signals on video recorders is a simple process that mirrors playback on standard audio recorders. The major concern in recovering audio signals is the ability to suppress the amplitude of signals as their frequency increases. For this reason the audio signal output is greater at lower frequencies. Left uncorrected the output volume would swing high and low as the audio playback frequency changes. To prevent this, the playback audio signal is passed through an equalization circuit that boosts the head output by an amount equal to that of the head loss. The result is an equal or "flat" response over the entire range of head playback frequencies.

THE PLAYBACK SERVO SYSTEM

In the playback mode there is no guarantee that an input video signal will be provided to the recorder. Therefore, the recorder's servo system must be able to operate without the aid of an incoming vertical sync reference. To achieve stable playback, the recorder switches its reference to a different set of reference pulses. Remember that the key element of a good video playback signal is the ability of the video head to completely read the video track without drifting into the guard band area. The operation of the playback cylinder servo is similar to that of the cylinder servo in the record mode. A 30 Hz signal, generated from a 3.58-MHz crystal found in the color circuit, serves as the vertical sync reference for the cylinder. (See Figure 5.11.) During playback, the cylinder PG pulse serves a dual function. It serves not only as the variable servo reference, but also as a switching signal for the head amplifiers. Previously, we talked about the need to switch the video heads on and off during playback. This is accomplished by using the cylinder PG pulse which is the most accurate method of determining video position. During the record mode the cylinder servo is

set so that both video heads contact the tape within a period no greater than 6.5 lines ahead of vertical sync. This is possible because the physical tape wrap around the head cylinder is greater than 180°. During playback, the cylinder head switching pulse is set to change phase to provide a continuous noise-free signal.

The playback capstan servo is referenced to a pre-recorded control track pulse. During recording, control track pulses are reflections of the vertical sync. Regardless of how perfect this process is in the record mode, during playback tape stretch can cause the positioning of this pulse to change. In order to guarantee that tapes recorded on one unit can be played back on another, the control track pulse is compared to the capstan frequency generator. During playback, the capstan frequency generator, which was used as the variable reference for the record servo, becomes the fixed reference and the control track pulse becomes the variable. Since the position of the control pulse is subject to tape inconsistencies and variations in the recorder transport, it is passed through a variable positioning circuit before being compared to the capstan frequency generator. This circuit is known as the Tracking Control, and is an operator adjusted control on the front panel of the recorder.

CONCLUSION

In this chapter we have looked at the record and playback processes of videotape recorders. Chapter 6 focuses on recorder maintenance and repair.

6 Preventive Maintenance of the Videotape Recorder

In any electro-mechanical device, the electronics are usually far more reliable than the mechanics. Troubleshooting procedures for videotape recorder transports usually begin with the mechanics and finish with the electronics, since the transports are dependent upon mechanical components such as rubber items, brakes and motors, which wear down or stop performing under continuous operating conditions. Most manufacturers recommend that these items be checked within the first 1000 hours of operation and be replaced after 1500 hours. The need for mechanical component replacement will usually occur due to wear; as such, it is usually a good idea to check the condition of your equipment for wear, and make repairs when it is not in use.

Since portable recorders are subject to a greater degree of uncontrollable environmental conditions, they should be checked more often. Surprisingly, most manufacturers recommend cleaning periods after as little as 500 hours. Remember that cleaning periods will vary with operating conditions. Often, the first recommended component replacement is that of the video head. Most manufacturers guarantee that video head specifications will hold for a period of no greater than 1000 hours. Typically, most users will not notice any apparent difference in picture quality after the 1000-hour period, and will achieve usable head life of up to 3000 hours. However, in cases where consistent quality is required, the video head should be changed after 1000 hours.

The Correct Environment

Preventive maintenance begins by creating the conditions that will allow the recorder to operate for the longest periods of time. Recorders should operate under dust free and reasonable temperature conditions.

Dusting

Place the recorder in an area where it will not be subject to the accidental introduction of foreign substances, such as coffee and soft drinks. If the recorder is placed in an enclosure, make sure there is proper ventilation.

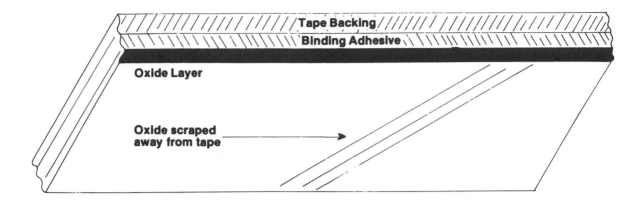

Figure 6.1: Oxide is scraped away from the tape backing with each pass of the video head.

The solutions offered by proper ventilation, however, can cause their own set of problems—dust and dirt. Care should be taken when dusting off recorders. Move the dust away from openings, such as air vents and the cassette housing. Dust falling into the recorder can fall on the transport, adhere to the tape and even clog the video head. Avoid using any furniture cleaners that can destroy plastic and cleaning sprays that can leak into the transport. The easiest way to avoid these problems is to use a cover to prevent dust from falling on the recorder. It also helps to keep the recorder covered when it is not in use.

Temperature Swings

Large temperature swings cause the recorder's rubber components to expand and contract. This results in the loss of their original shape and uneven tape transport. Prolonged operation under air conditioning is not always the answer and low humidity conditions can cause rubber to dry up and crack. Manufacturers recommend that recorders be operated within a humidity range of 60% to 70%. Temperature ranges should not be greater than 40° Celsius (104° Fahrenheit). It is important to remember that operating temperature requirements include both the recorder's internal and external temperatures. The recorder's internal electronic components, particularly the power transformer, generate a lot of heat. For this reason, the recorder can begin to act erratic when outside temperatures reach the mid-90s.

THE IMPORTANCE OF VIDEOTAPE CARE

Videotape care also plays a critical role in recorder maintenance. Each time the tape passes in front of the video head, oxide is scraped from the tape backing. This process can continue during each pass until the recording surface is completely scraped away. (See Figure 6.1.) At this point, the loose oxide dust particles can fasten themselves to head surfaces and rubber drive elements such as the pinch roller. Left unchecked, the oxide particles can completely clog the video head gap, causing a lack of tape-to-head contact, resulting in signal loss.

Polishing

The microscopic iron oxide elements that adhere to the rubber components cause friction and wear. The condition caused by such con-

Figure 6.2: Worn pinch roller exhibits shiny surface.

tinuous wear is called polishing and results in shiny areas on the rubber components. (See Figure 6.2.)

As the rubber drive elements that contact the tape become contaminated by tape oxides, the component surfaces, such as the impedance rollers and capstan pinch roller, lose their contact with the tape. As a result, the tape slips and the timing relationship between the video head and videotape track is lost. This condition looks like mistracking, but cannot be corrected by adjusting the recorder's tracking control. As more tape oxide builds up, the opposite condition can occur. This is particularly true when the tape contacts moisture. The tape can adhere to a component surface such as the video head or the capstan pinch roller. In either case, the tape is destroyed. However, if the videotape adheres to the head cylinder it can break the video heads.

Clogging the Head Gap

While the wearing of transport components is a gradual process, head clogging is not. The head gap, where signals are transferred between the head and the tape, varies in width between 1 micron and 0.3 micron. Only small amounts of oxide are required to clog the head gap and reduce signal output to zero. Before this occurs, oxide particles that adhere to the head surfaces will cause a loss of contact between head and tape. The loss of this intimate contact results in a loss of signal quality. The condition looks like black streaks or tape dropout in the playback picture. (See Figure 6.3.)

Tape Life

In general, most videotapes can achieve at least 200 normal passes. As the tape approaches its maximum usage time, its signal should be copied onto a fresh tape, and the old tape discarded. Remember that the number of good passes a tape can make is dependent upon its usage. Playing back tapes in the still mode or fast scan viewing modes further increases wear and lowers useful tape life.

There are a number of steps you can take to ensure maximum tape life and minimum recorder damage. These are listed below:

1. Due to shipping, new videotapes are usually packed loosely around their hubs. In addition, vibrations encountered in shipping can loosen oxide particles. Loosely wound

Figure 6.3: Playback with a dirty head.

tapes that are placed directly in a recorder will be damaged due to stretching; the recorder will be damaged due to loose oxide. Before using a new tape, run it through the recorder in the fast-forward and reverse modes. This process is known as "packing" (or "shuttling"), and tightens the tape around the hubs. It also causes loose oxide to fall away from the tape surface.

2. Observe the quality of the playback video. Noise specks that cannot be cleared up by adjustment of the tracking control (dropout), can be a result of oxide loss. Excessive tape dropouts indicate that the tape should be discarded, and the transport cleaned.

3. As an operator, you can determine when tapes should be discarded by physically in-

specting them over periodic usage. This is done by releasing the cover lock on the videotape cassette, which enables you to flip open the cassette to expose the videotape. The tape should be inspected in two locations—along the edges to see if there are any creases and in the middle for scratches. Creases indicate that the tape is running too high or too low along the transport. If a creased tape is kept in use, it can fold under itself and damage the video head. Scratches, sometimes referred to as head scarring, are a result of video head-to-tape pressure. While it can be an indication of a recorder problem, this condition will also result from excessive playback in the still mode. In either case, since so much oxide has been loosened from the tape, it should be discarded.

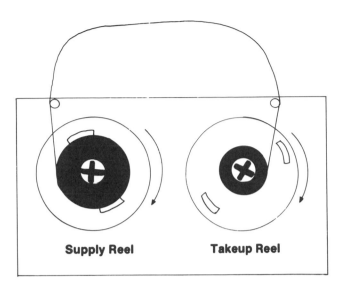

Figure 6.4: The tape travels from the supply reel to the take-up reel.

4. If visual inspection of the tape does not yield either of the two conditions noted above, but the video head continues to clog with repeated use of an individual tape, discard the tape anyway, to avoid the risk of a head clog that cannot be corrected by cleaning.

VIDEOTAPE MECHANICS

Slow loss of recorder signal quality over a period of time, or inconsistent recording, can often be an indication of the need for preventive maintenance. To the untrained technician, these problems can first appear to be caused by defective electronics. Don't be fooled. By taking this approach time and money can be wasted if you replace a perfectly good component. Don't attempt to re-adjust the electronics as a solution to mechanical problems. If you are successful, it will only serve to mask the problems for a short period of time until additional wear occurs.

OPERATION OF THE TAPE TRANSPORT SYSTEM

Good tape-to-head contact, and tape interchangeability are the two primary responsibilities of the tape transport system. Good tape-to-head contact is important because playback signals come off the tape at extremely low levels. These signal amplitudes must be great enough to be read by the playback processing circuits. In the record mode, signals are placed on the tape at low levels. Misalignment of the transport, which results in lack of tape contact, can cause lower than normal recording levels. If this occurs, the heads will have a harder time reading the signal off of the tape during playback. Misalignment, therefore, becomes a two-fold problem for both the recording and playback processes by causing amplification of noise in the signal and unacceptable playback.

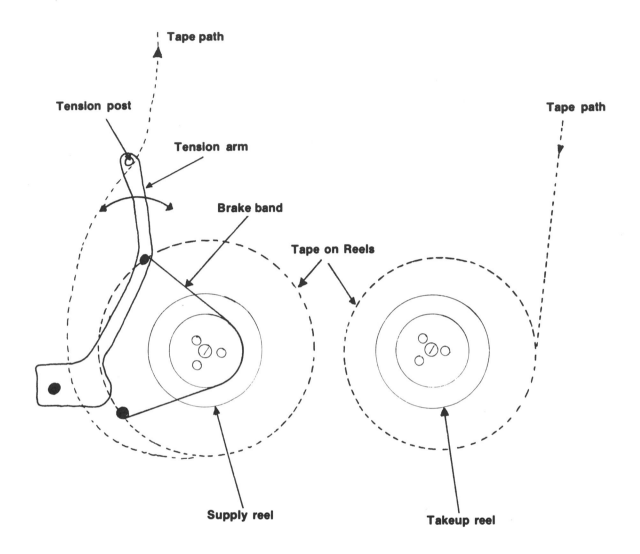

Figure 6.5: Back tension regulation.

IDENTIFYING TRANSPORT COMPONENTS

Before you attempt to adjust recorder mechanics, you should become familiar with the various components that make up the tape transport system. (See Chapter 7 for an in-depth discussion of videotape recorder adjustments.)

The Supply Reel

Regardless of the format of the video recorder, tape is always fed from the supply reel to the take-up reel in the record and playback modes. (See Figure 6.4.) As such, the order by which each head is contacted is the same regardless of format. The transport process begins when the tape is pulled from the supply

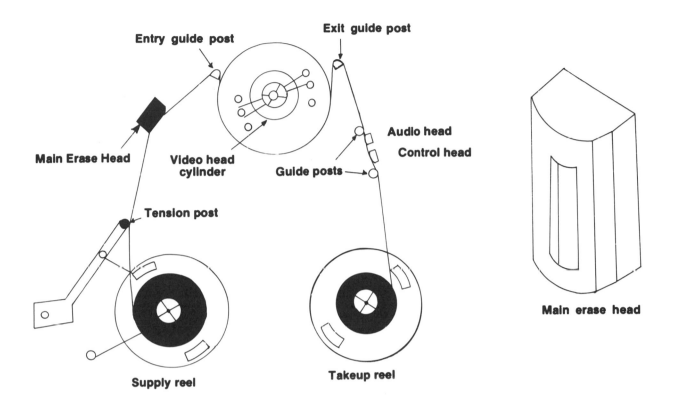

Figure 6.6: Tape path including main erase head, video head cylinder, audio and control heads, and guide posts.

reel to the take-up reel. In order to maintain a constant tape speed during playback and recording, it is necessary that the tension exhibited by the supply reel remain constant despite changes in the amount of tape it is holding. A braking band wrapped around the supply reel table maintains constant tension. (The reel "tables" are spindles or platforms on which the tape reels rest.) This band, called the "back tension" band, increases its pressure around the supply reel table as its tape load diminishes. The increase in back tension band pressure, along with the decrease in supply reel tape load, results in a constant tension on the take-up reel.

The position of the supply reel varies across formats. For example, if you stand in front of a 3/4-inch U-Matic recorder, the supply reel will be located on the right side. In a VHS recorder, the supply reel will be found on the left side. In any case, identification of the starting point for tape transport is easy once you locate the back tension band. (See Figure 6.5.)

Full Erase Head

Prior to recording on tape, it is necessary to erase any previously recorded signals that may be on the tape. As noted, signals are recorded on tape at extremely low levels. Signal strength at these low levels is not strong enough to re-align the tape to accept new signals. As such, the first head that the tape contacts after leaving the supply reel is the full erase head (see Figure 6.6). During the record mode as the tape moves past the erase head, a high amplitude, high frequency signal is applied to the tape. This signal magnetically moves the metal oxide content of the tape to a position where it can readily accept new signals.

Upper Drum

As the tape travels along the tape path, it contacts the upper drum assembly where the rotating video heads record the signal on the tape. The tape is positioned around the upper drum by a series of "guide posts." Those guide posts located along the tape path before it reaches the upper drum are entrance guide posts; those contacting the tape after the signal has been recorded are exit guide posts. (See Figure 6.6.)

Audio and Control Heads

The audio and control track signals are the last to be applied to the tape. These signals are applied by two stationary heads that are joined closely together (or combined). They are located along the tape path after the tape has exited the upper cylinder.

The tape is positioned against the audio/control track head by a guide post located on its exit side. (See Figure 6.7.) If the recorder has an audio dub feature, it will have an audio-only erase head positioned ahead of the audio and control heads.

Capstan and Pinch Roller

After all the signals have been applied to the tape, it reaches the capstan shaft and pinch roller. The capstan is a metal shaft that is attached either directly (direct-drive capstan) or via a belt (belt-driven capstan) to a motor. A rubber pinch roller evenly forces the tape against the shaft, causing it to travel at a constant speed along an even plane. (See Figure 6.8.)

The Take-Up Reel

Finally, the tape reaches the take-up reel, which is driven by a set of pulleys. In order to avoid tape spillage, which would damage the tape, the rate of tape take up by the take-up reel must equal the rate of tape fed to it by the capstan and pinch roller assemblies.

The correct movement of the tape is only half of the equation. Once proper tape transport has been achieved, the signal must be read by the video head.

THE VIDEO HEAD

Since the video head is the primary component for determining signal quality, it is usually the one most subject to user contact. Although head life can extend between 1000 and 3000 hours, head replacement will usually be the result of abuse, rather than normal wear. Video head preventive maintenance follows the same pattern as that for the video recorder. Start with the environment and then move to the videotape. As the tape is in direct and constant contact with the video head, the quality of the tape will have a direct affect on head life. Stay with the known brands of tape. The major difference in the quality of tape is the polishing of the oxide coating. Low-quality tapes have low density coatings that have a tendency to shed, causing video head damage. Saving a few dollars on videotape could cost you a video head replacement. Remember to keep a record of tape usage and the number of times you dub signals onto a fresh tape, as tape usage approaches 200 passes.

Head Cleaning and Head Replacement

More often than not, video head replacement results from damage due to over cleaning, rather than wear. Avoid the common urge to frequently clean the video heads. Any type of contact with the video head can lead to the possibility of head damage. In order to eliminate the human factor, many users clean video heads with a head cleaning tape. Since these

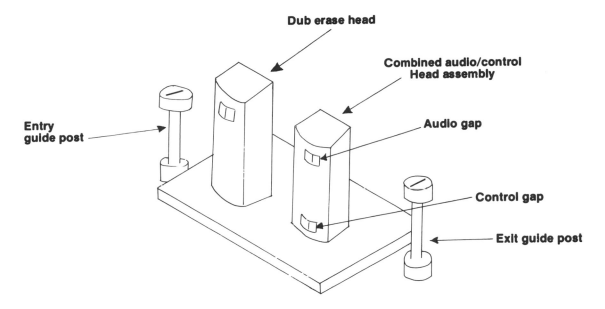

Figure 6.7: The audio/control head and dubbing erase head are stationary. The guide posts position the tape.

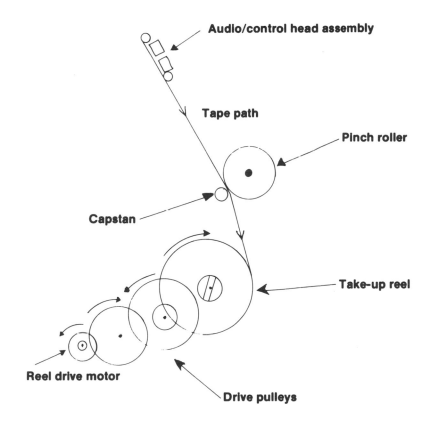

Figure 6.8: Tape finishing its path back to the take-up reel.

tapes operate by scraping dirt away from the head surface, they also contribute to a loss of head protrusion. As such, overuse of the cleaning cassette can actually promote head wear and lead to more frequent head replacements. The type of material used in the cleaning cassette, along with the method of cleaning, can have a great affect on head wear. Use head cleaning cassettes with non-woven, low abrasive materials. In addition, cleaning cassettes that use a wetting solution decrease tape-to-head friction. Just remember to use the wetting solution or irreversible head damage can occur. Most of all, limit the use of the cleaning tape by using it only when the playback picture is noisy.

Cleaning the Video Heads: Direct Method

While use of a cleaning tape helps to eliminate the human factor, it is possible that extremely clogged heads will not be cleared up by using the cleaning tape. Although the direct cleaning method ensures direct contact between video head and cleaner, done improperly, it could be the cause of head breakage and clogging.

Make sure you select an applicator that will not leave lint that might lead to head clogging. Many video stores sell special head cleaning tabs that are lint free. Use a freon based solution as a cleaner, since it evaporates under low-temperature and leaves no residue. The ability of the freon to evaporate under low-temperature is important in preventing recorder damage. If any moisture is left around the cylinder, it could cause the tape to ''seize,'' destroying both the video heads and the tape. (For this reason avoid using alcohol.)

Clean the video heads by moving the cleaning tab across the surface of the video head in one direction. Back and forth movement can cause the edge of the video head to scrape against the cleaning tab and loosen lint. Avoid any up and down movement. The video head is very strong against pressure applied across its surface and fragile to pressure applied to its top and bottom surfaces.

Finding the Source of the Clog

After cleaning the video heads, it's time to determine the source of the clog. Do not insert the tape you played prior to the head clog. If it was the source of your problem, you'll be back to square one and will have to start the cleaning process over. Use a fresh tape, make a recording and check the playback. If the playback is good with the fresh tape, check the recorder's playback with the previously recorded tape. If the playback is good, but the tape has a number of hours on it, suspect the tape and make a dub the first chance you get. If the playback begins with a good picture, but then turns to snow, it's an indication that the video head is chipped. Video heads can crack or chip in areas other than the head gap. When it occurs, the video head can still produce a picture, but the chip will scrape oxide from the tape and clog the head. If after cleaning the video heads, the picture output is still zero, chances are the heads are broken. In either of the latter two cases, the video head will probably have to be replaced.

Video head replacement and adjustments and alignment of videotape recorders are discussed in Chapter 7.

7 Adjustment and Alignment of the Videotape Recorder

In Chapter 6, we discussed preventive maintenance of the videotape recorder. However, even with the best of care, the VTR, which is largely a mechanical device, is subject to wear. All rubber parts, video heads, guide posts, etc. can wear to the point that the machine becomes useless. With the replacement of worn parts comes the task of mechanical alignment. Electronic circuit components can also change their value so occasional electronic adjustments may also be required. In this chapter we will examine adjustments and alignments that can be made to the videotape recorder.

Although videotape recorders differ from format to format (as well as within like formats), the generic nature of their design will enable us to interpret problems, locate key test points, read waveforms and make repairs. This generic design is based on the common principles and theory of magnetic tape recording covered in Chapter 2. Before we expand on these concepts, however, it is necessary to cover two points that should be taken into consideration before making repairs to any piece of video equipment. First, understand the common op-

eration of the equipment in question by reading the unit's operation manual. This will help you to understand the unit's operating limitations, and will point out any peculiar "problems" that can be the result of the unit's normal operation. Second, make sure you have all the necessary tools and test equipment. This includes not only the common repair test equipment, such as an oscilloscope, but also any particular items that the manufacturer requires, including the unit's service manual. (While the information provided in this book can serve as a general guide to the repair of video equipment, for maximum efficiency it should be used in conjunction with the manufacturer's service manual, which will provide the location of specific test points and alignment procedures.)

TAPE TRANSPORT ADJUSTMENTS

There are three goals to maintain when repairing or adjusting tape transports. These are:

1. The even and uninhibited transport of the tape around the cylinder that results in no tape damage.

2. Maximum tape-to-head contact, to achieve maximum signal transfer to and from the tape.
3. Interchangeability, so that tapes recorded on one unit can be played on another unit of the same format.

To achieve interchangeability between recorders of the same format it is necessary to make all mechanical adjustments to a standard. To meet these conditions, manufacturers provide ''standard alignment tapes'' for each format. These tapes are recorded on special units in Japan that are constantly monitored to ensure that the transports do not go out of tolerance. The signals recorded on these tapes are designed to test the important video, audio and servo parameters of recorders within a particular format. Because video head width, as well as the electronic position of the head switching pulse, can vary on recorders within a given format, a VHS, Beta or U-Matic standard alignment tape will not necessarily work on all models. It is important to consult your recorder's service manual for the specific number of the alignment tape to be used with that recorder.

Costs for these alignment tapes can range from $200 to $300. Because of this high cost, it is recommended that any time you use a standard tape, you first check the recorder's physical transport condition by using an expendable tape (just in case the recorder chews it up).

Checking Tape-to-Head Contact

Stationary Heads

Stationary heads—the full erase head and control track/audio heads—contact the base of the lower cylinder. Adjustment of these heads is usually only performed when the heads are replaced. This procedure involves the physical positioning of each new video head, as well as fine adjustments to the entrance and exit guide posts to ensure maximum contact with the drum cylinder.

Tape Transport Adjustments

Replacement of transport components such as the rubber idlers, the back tension band or reel tables requires the removal of the cassette housing. Removing any part of the transport that directly affects tape contact will require adjustment of the tape transport.

To begin, remove the recorder's outer casing. Most new recorders also contain a shield or circuit board over the video head which prevents RF transmissions, such as over-the-air television and radio signals, from being picked up by the wiring of the upper cylinder and amplified by the recorder electronics. Remove this shield, taking care not to drop the holding screws into the transport. If the cassette lid blocks your view of the first tape contact points (such as the full erase head), it too must be removed. To inspect the condition of the back tension band, remove the entire cassette housing. Remember that the cassette lid and housing are responsible for holding the videocassette in its proper position. When you load the cassette without either of these components, it is necessary to use some external device to compensate for the loss of tension. Failure to do so can result in the tape running off of the guide posts and damaging the video head. To avoid this, most manufacturers provide a pressure bar in their repair kits.

Next, confirm that the transport mechanism exhibits no problems during tape loading. If the transport pulls at the tape or loads unevenly without a smooth motion, there is probably a supply reel problem. After the cassette is loaded, confirm that the tape is being transported from the supply reel to the take-up reel. The tape should make good contact with each of the guide posts. (See Figure 7.1.) There should be no slack or creases in the tape caused by its riding too high or low on the guide post (see Figure 7.2). If an adjustment needs to be made, turn the guide post until the tape is riding directly in the middle of the roller (see Figure 7.3). In addition, make sure that each of the rollers is turning smoothly. Next observe the tape as it crosses each of the stationary heads.

7.1: The tape moves smoothly along its path, making contact with each of the guide posts.

The tape must make contact with each of the heads, while maintaining a parallel and flat position against the head. If the tape position is not parallel, the azimuth of the head must be adjusted. if the tape is not positioned flat against the head, the tilt of the head must be adjusted.

In the case of the VHS control track/audio head (CTL/audio) the control track is recorded on the bottom section of the tape and the audio is recorded on the top section. The guide posts must position the tape so that it crosses both sections of each of the heads. Also, in order to achieve maximum signal transfer, the tape must run parallel along the complete length of the individual head (see Figure 7.4).

Physical tape guidance around the lower drum cylinder is a little harder to eyeball for rough adjustments. Prior to loading the tape,

look for the tape guide edge in the lower cylinder section (see Figures 7.5 and 7.6). The entrance and exit guide posts must be adjusted so the tape will ride smoothly on the guide post and within the groove of the lower cylinder. This will ensure that the video head will make contact with the tape for the complete period of time it takes to record one video field. While the guide posts are meant to be adjusted, avoid loosening the screws that hold them to the base. This adjustment is preset at the factory. A change could result in a reduction of signal quality.

After the guide posts have been adjusted, recheck the tape flow. If it appears to be smooth, move on to the tape tension adjustments. Tape tension is primarily controlled by a felt band that is wrapped around the supply reel and connected to a metal post that contacts

Figure 7.2: Tape riding too low on the guide post.

Figure 7.3: Tape riding in the middle of the guide post roller.

Figure 7.4: Tape maintains parallel position flat against the head.

the tape as it leaves the supply reel (see Figure 7.7). As the tape moves from the supply reel to the take-up reel, the pressure against the post changes because of the transfer of bulk weight. This change of pressure causes the tension band to loosen or tighten its hold around the supply reel. At the beginning of a recording (or playback), when most of the tape is on the supply reel, the tension band loosens. As the tape is transferred to the take-up reel, the tension band tightens to maintain consistent tape tension. Without a back tension band, the physical position of the tape, as its bulk weight is moved from the supply reel to the take-up reel, changes with tape load. The degree of lack of tape tension can result in one of two problems.

1. Minor distortions can change the pitch of video tracks, which in turn can cause a misalignment of the horizontal sync of the video tracks (a bending of the video picture below the head switching point). As the back tension error increases, the bending moves into the next frame where it appears at the top of the picture. This bending is known as skew error.

2. Under extreme conditions, the tape can lose contact with the video heads, beginning at the cylinder entrance point. In most recorders this will appear as a band of noise that cannot be cleared up by the tracking control. (Some U-Matic recorders blank out the screen when the FM playback level drops below a certain level.)

BACK TENSION ADJUSTMENT

Because the signals are positioned on the tape differently for each video format, each format has a different back tension requirement. Different manufacturers will also have

Figure 7.5: Note guide edge in lower cylinder section.

Figure 7.6: Tape riding smoothly along guide edge.

Supply reel   Back tension band   Take-up reel

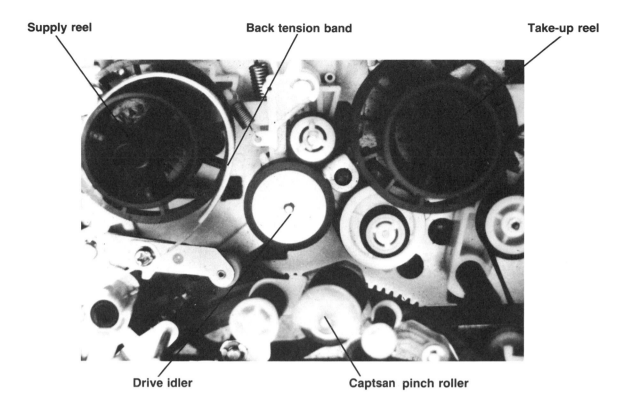

Drive idler   Captsan pinch roller

Figure 7.7: Face-up view of the recorder displays back tension band, drive idler and capstan pinch roller.

their own acceptable tolerance levels, so it's a good idea to consult the recorder's service manual before beginning adjustments. In general, 1/2-inch consumer and industrial recorders have a fixed back tension for playback. Three-quarter inch recorders have an operator control (skew control) that varies the back tension in playback. When checking U-Matic back tension make sure that the skew control is in its mid-point position.

The Tentelometer

The Tentelometer, manufactured by Tentel, is most often used to measure back tension. Because of the physical differences between 1/2-inch and 3/4-inch tape, the Tentelometers used to adjust each format are different and cannot be interchanged.

To check back tension, place the Tentelome-

ter on the entrance side of the transport, between the full erase head and entrance guide post. Make sure that all three posts of the meter make good contact with the tape. Position the meter so that it is exactly vertical and parallel to the tape path. Using the most common lengths of tape, T-120 for VHS, L-500 for Beta and a 60-minute tape for U-Matic, check that back tension remains constant at the beginning, middle and end of the tape. If the back tension readings for these three sections of tape do not meet the manufacturer's requirements, adjustment or replacement of the back tension band might be necessary.

Because U-Matic recorders contain an operator skew control, many service manuals call out the measurements for skew control minimum and maximum settings. In addition, U-Matic recorders used in editing systems, which must maintain transport accuracy in their visual scan modes, call for the measurement of take-up tension as well as back tension. To perform measurements in various take-up modes, place the Tentelometer between the exit guide posts and the audio/control track head.

After the rough transport adjustments have been completed and you have confirmed, once again, that the transfer of tape between the supply reel and the take-up reel is smooth, you can begin to fine tune the system.

FINE TUNING THE TRANSPORT SYSTEM

The key to the good performance of any VCR is its ability to play back a properly recorded signal. Any point where the videotape does not make contact with the stationary head or video heads will result in a deficiency in the playback FM waveform, and distortion in the playback picture.

Using the Standard Alignment Tape

To adjust the recorder's transport to a standard, you must use a tape that has been recorded on a properly adjusted standard transport (the standard alignment tape). The standard alignment tape provides a properly recorded FM signal that will help you to determine the source of problems in a faulty VCR. The playback FM waveform must be a close reproduction of the record current that is fed to the video head during the recording process. The only difference between the two waveforms should be a slight dip in the playback waveform caused by playback video head switching.

Viewing the FM Playback Waveform

To view the playback FM waveform, it is necessary to use a dual channel oscilloscope. Since the head-switching pulse, which is created by the recorder's servo system, is responsible for turning on and off the head playback amplifiers, it makes an excellent oscilloscope trigger pulse for observing the output of the playback FM signal.

Setting Up the Oscilloscope

Set up the oscilloscope by displaying the head switching pulse on one of the scope channels. Adjust the display so the change-over point falls on the center graticule of the scope. Remember to use this channel as your trigger scope reference. Connect the other scope channel to the output of the video head amplifier. Most manufacturers provide test points for both the head switching and FM signals. The output from each of the heads will be displayed in each half of the scope faceplate.

Reading the FM Waveform

After the oscilloscope is properly set up, the FM waveform can be read like a book (see Figure 7.8). The left side of each envelope represents the entrance point; the right side represents the exit point. First confirm that the operator tracking control is in the detent position and that it represents the maximum FM head output. You can confirm this by turning the tracking control away from the detent position. If the FM waveform drops then you know it was in the correct position. Next, compare the signal level on the scope with the level given in the unit's service manual. In general, if the highest level achieved is no greater than 60% of the level indicated in the manual, the video head should be replaced.

Our readings begin with a check of the overall quality of the FM envelope. Begin by confirming that the output from each head is free of fluctuations. If the entire envelope is rising and falling at an even rate, chances are that the recorder has a servo problem. Either the capstan or the head cylinder is running off speed causing the video heads to cross between the video tracks and the guard band. The FM waveform will rise and fall depending on the amount of video or guard band information the head is reading. This problem can also be visually confirmed on a monitor, where the playback picture will exhibit noise that corresponds to the decreasing FM information.

The cause of distortions, as they relate to

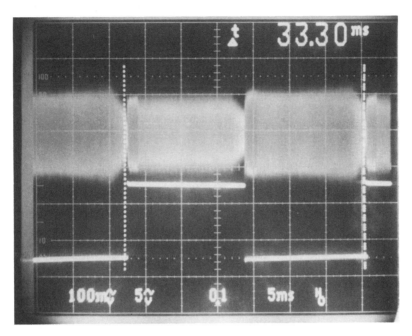

Figure 7.8: FM output as viewed on an oscilloscope.

the transport, can be read right off the oscilloscope. Those on the left side of the waveform indicate entrance problems; those on the right are signs of exit problems. If the waveform shows distortions at both ends, then both the entrance and exit tape paths must be checked.

Flattening Out the FM Waveform

The tape guide posts located closest to the entrance and exit head cylinder points have the greatest effect on the FM waveform. Adjust each of these posts until the waveform is flat and exhibits no blank spacing either within an individual envelope or between both head envelopes. Because the FM envelope recorded on the standard alignment tape is of such a high signal level, distortions cannot always be seen with the tracking control set to the detent position. Lower the FM envelope by moving the tracking control in either direction from the detent position, and confirm that the en-

velope remains flat, with no distortion on either of its sides, as it approaches its minimum level. Should any section of the FM waveform change as the envelope decreases, re-adjust the approach guide post so the entire envelope will remain flat from its minimum to maximum levels. Remember that we are only looking for distortion *within* the individual waveform. If each of the outputs from the heads is flat, but is of a different level, the upper head cylinder may need to be mechanically repositioned. (This adjustment is usually necessary when the video heads are replaced.)

CONTROL/AUDIO HEAD ADJUSTMENTS

The repositioning of the primary entrance and exit guide posts has the greatest effect on tape contact with the video head cylinder. However, as the tape path is continuous, no guide post can be adjusted independent of the others. Therefore, the adjustment of one pri-

CTL/Audio control track adjustment

Figure 7.9: Screw for adjusting audio/control position.

mary guide post usually requires that all the others be checked. If a properly adjusted primary guide post results in tape curling on the others, reposition them to correct this condition, and then reposition each of the stationary heads for good tape contact. This final positioning of the stationary heads will ensure that audio, control and FM outputs are maximized.

Video head signal output is not only dependent on good tape contact, but also on the amount of time the contact occurs. As previously noted, even if the video head makes good tape contact at a point where a guard band has been "recorded," the overall output will be distorted. The reading of the control pulse off the tape controls the tape speed, and is designed to allow the video head to read the center of the video track. Physical vertical positioning of the tape will determine initial contact, while

horizontal positioning along the tape path will determine the time period during which the control pulse will be read. In addition, the CTL head casing houses the audio head. So adjusting the audio/control position (see Figure 7.9) becomes a compromise between maximum audio, control track pulse output and FM video head output. Use the oscilloscope to observe these signals after their first stage of amplification. You may find that this adjustment becomes a bit of a compromise as the maximum setting for one signal may not yield the best signal output for the other.

VIDEO HEAD REPLACEMENT

To maintain good signal transfer, the video head must make close contact with the tape. The degree of contact between the videotape

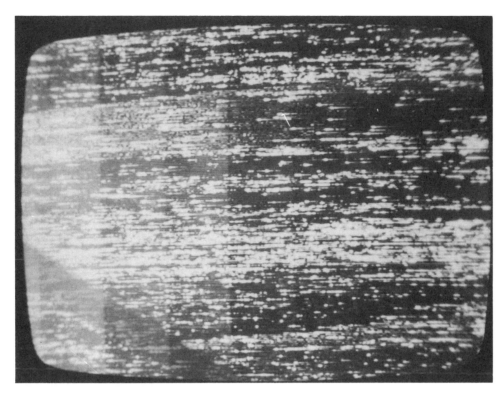

Figure 7.10: Snow in the playback picture.

and the video head is referred to as tip projection or protrusion. As the tape contacts the head's surface, the tip area, which houses the video head gap, will wear down and lose its ability to contact the tape. When this happens much of the signal energy needed to write and read the FM signal is lost in the "free space" area between the tape and the head. To the viewer, the playback picture appears to have a lot of snow (see Figure 7.10). If turning the recorder's tracking control in either direction worsens the condition, the problem is most likely head wear. This problem is usually more noticeable during the playback of a self-recording then it is during the playback of a pre-recorded tape because signal losses occur both during the recording and playback processes.

Head protrusion loss is usually referred to in terms of microns, although most measuring devices use a scale of ten-thousandths of an inch. Typically, video heads can wear down to 70% of their original protrusion and still record and playback good quality signals. Marginally acceptable pictures can be realized at 30% of new head protrusion. Head wear below this figure will almost certainly result in the need for head replacement.

How often you replace your video heads is a direct function of the application of your equipment. The need to maintain high-quality recordings will mandate that the video heads be replaced more often.

Removing the Video Head

Video head replacement requires a series of

interrelated mechanical and electronic adjustments. Consult the manufacturer's service manual, then assemble the test equipment which should include an oscilloscope, a protrusion or concentricity gauge and the manufacturer's test tape.

The upper drum cylinder (see Figure 7.11), which houses the video heads, is mechanically attached to the drum assembly by a pair of set-screws. The individual heads are electronically attached to the rest of the recorder's electronics by a series of wires. These wires mate to those of the upper rotary transformer at a junction point that serves as a hub for the head cylinder. Desolder the head wires prior to loosening the head set-screws. When the head set-screws are removed, the head cylinder is set free. As a result, any pressure on the upper cylinder can cause the video head to press against the lower cylinder and break. First loosen each screw to maintain equal pressure on both sides of the head cylinder. Refer to the manufacturer's service manual for complete instruction on head removal. When removing the head, handle it with care. You can never be sure that the video head is the source of your problem until you have successfully changed it. Rough treatment during removal can cause damage to a perfectly good head.

When removing the upper drum cylinder, place your fingers at a 90° angle to the video heads. Remember that any pressure against the video heads can break them. Pull the upper head cylinder straight up. If the cylinder fit is tight, gently rock it back and forth. Take care not to rock the head too much or the head may break against the lower cylinder.

Mount the new head cylinder. Remember, no matter how tight the upper cylinder is, never apply force. Tighten the head set-screws by alternately turning each one so each side of the cylinder falls into place evenly. Resolder the head wires and dress them down against the surface of the upper cylinder.

ADJUSTING THE VIDEO HEAD

Again, the ability of the video heads to write and read signals is dependent on the heads making maximum contact with the tape. Any loss of tape contact will result in a loss of signal quality. Each individual video head must record each video track (each video field) at the same angle or pitch. Any change in the physical position of the head will result in a different contact point and thereby reduce signal output. Basically, there are two requirements for good and equal head-to-tape contact.

1. Each of the video heads must be of equal distance from the tape.
2. Each of the video heads must intersect the videotape at the same point along the video track.

At the factory, each video head is mounted on the cylinder on the same plane and at the same distance from the cylinder surface. The process of mounting the video heads to the cylinder is so difficult that it is impossible to replace just one of the video heads. The equipment used during the manufacture of the head cylinder produces the best signal results by performing the final tuning adjustments during head set-up. Even if one of the video heads breaks, a new cylinder, containing two video heads, must be used as a replacement. When the new upper head drum is mounted to the lower cylinder, the amount of pressure applied to each of the set-screws can offset the parameters required for good video reproduction: The drum needs to be concentric for equal head protrusion, and the height of each head must be the same for equal tape contact.

Setting Head Protrusion

To begin the fine adjustment procedure, set the head protrusion measurement. Because the heads have been pre-set at the factory to have equal protrusion, successful adjustment consists of achieving concentricity of the upper drum cylinder around the center hub. Since the cylinder can be removed from the center hub, it is possible that fixing the upper cylinder can cause both heads to have unequal protrusion. This condition creates two problems: The head with the lesser protrusion reads and writes

Grounding or anti-static brush

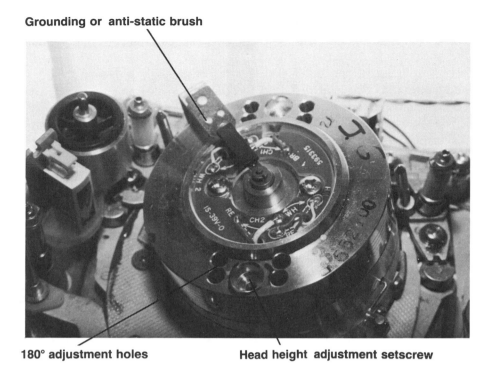

180° adjustment holes   Head height adjustment setscrew

Figure 7.11: View of the upper head cylinder.

FM signals at lower amplitudes, making equal head amplitude impossible. And, the head with the greatest amount of protrusion presses into the videotape causing head wear. The result will be poor head output with a shorter than normal head life. It is this latter condition that dictates that head protrusion be checked regardless of the type of upper drum cylinder. The adjustment is done by using a gauge that measures the concentricity of the upper drum cylinder. By loosening the head set-screws, the upper drum should be adjusted to show a difference of no greater that ± 1.5 mm.

Setting the Head Height

Follow the head protrusion adjustment by setting the head height. A difference in height between the two heads will cause the heads to physically cross the video tracks at different positions. As in the case of differences in head protrusion, the differences in head height between the two heads will result in an imbalance of FM output. This difference is best displayed in the PAUSE mode. When head height differs each head will cross into the guard band at a different location on the video track. The pause playback picture shows two separate bands of noise. An increase in picture noise content means that there is a reduction of picture video signal. To adjust for equal head height, input the head switching pulse and the FM output signal from the head switching amplifier into an oscilloscope. Reference the oscilloscope to the head switching pulse and uncalibrate the scope to display the output from each head on each side of the center graticle. In the STILL mode, the change in tape pitch will cause the video head to cross into the guard band region at some point during its contact with the video track. On the oscilloscope, the FM waveform will appear as a diamond shape. The highest signal amplitude represents maximum contact with the recorded track, while the minimum FM signal represents the point where the video head reads the maximum amount of guard band. Differences in head height will cause these peaks and valleys to occur at different positions from the starting point of the FM envelope.

To adjust for proper head height, select one head to serve as the reference and the other as the head to be adjusted. Mark the video head to be adjusted. (This step is important as the goal of the adjustment is to achieve equal head height. Back and forth adjustment between the two heads can only result in confusion.) With the recorder in the STOP mode, turn the head height adjustment screw (refer to Figure 7.11) no more than a quarter turn. Play back the standard tape in the STILL mode, and observe both the video output picture and FM waveform. As the video heads move into alignment, the output picture will show the noise bands moving together, while the peaks and valleys of the FM waveform will also move into alignment. Due to the various ways by which monitors can exhibit the differences in head height, they should be used only as a back-up check to the FM waveform. Remember to take great care turning the head height adjustment screw. Too much pressure on the head will bend the metal and the head will have to be replaced.

Head Diherial

The last physical head adjustment is head diherial. This adjustment insures that the video heads are positioned exactly 180° apart from each other. Since this adjustment is not affected by the remounting of the head set-screws, it is often the least required adjustment. Diherial offset usually occurs due to a manufacturing problem, or possible horizontal head movement during head height adjustments.

The physical displacement of the video heads means that the rate at which the signals are read off the tape will be different from the rate read by the monitor. This is particularly true of television sync signals. When the

monitor sync is disrupted after the head switching point, it could take a considerable amount of time to recover. When the monitor sees horizontal sync occurring at different times, the beam will move back and forth trying to meet the sync being received from the recorder. Vertical lines in the picture will separate from the head switching point and come together at some place in the active scan of the next frame. That point is determined by the monitor's horizontal automatic frequency control (HAFC). To correct this condition, manufacturers provide a series of holes to the left and right of the video head (refer to Figure 7.11). By inserting a small tool or screwdriver into the holes, the head can be pushed to the left or right. Again, as in the case of head height adjustment, use one head as the reference and adjust the other. Make sure to mark the adjusted head. Play back the monoscope pattern, usually found on all manufacturer's test tapes, and observe the separation of the vertical lines starting at the top of the picture. Adjust the head position until the lines move closer together.

THE DRIVE IDLER SYSTEM

The idler system is responsible for all tape loading and movement, which places this system under a great deal of stress. Most early idler drive systems relied on a series of main and immediate idlers for rewind, fast-forward and play functions. As scan functions became more common, and editing systems required greater accuracy for the shuttling of tape, transports developed in two directions. Low-cost recorders have replaced their multiple-drive systems with a single idler that rotates between the supply and take-up reels, depending on the mode. And, high-end recorders, particularly those used for industrial applications and in editing systems, use direct motors for the supply and take-up reels.

The reduced idler drive system of the low-end recorders has placed a greater strain on the system, often causing the components to wear at uneven rates. When this occurs, the idler can slip against the drive reel and cause irregular tape movement. Any blockage of tape

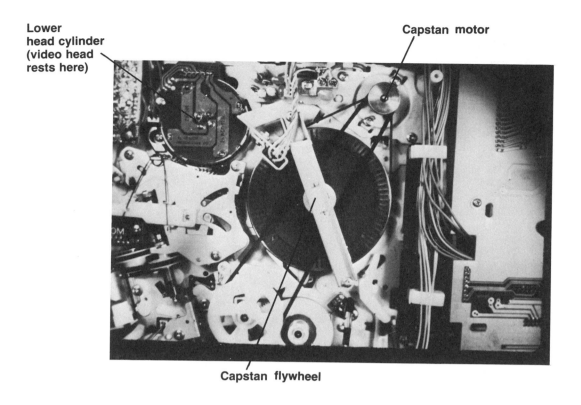

Figure 7.12: Recorder underside displays capstan flywheel and motor.

movement during loading or transport, for a period of five to eight seconds, will cause the recorder's fail safe system to activate and place the recorder in the STOP mode. If replacement parts are not readily available, you can try to clean the idlers with a soft cloth dampened with alcohol. Cleaning dirt away from the idler will improve tape contact and drive torque. Keep in mind that this solution is only temporary and the idler should be replaced as soon as possible.

CAPSTAN PRESSURE ROLLER AND DRIVE BELT

After the tape has been successfully loaded, the capstan pressure roller (pinch roller) controls the smooth movement of the tape by pressing it against the capstan shaft. While the pressure roller is a free-moving idler, the capstan is a driven element. Here again, the cost of

the recorder determines the method of drive. Low-cost recorders use a relay belt coupled to the capstan motor. High-end recorders use a direct-drive capstan motor that is connected directly to the shaft. As previously noted, these rubber components wear and the surfaces in contact with the drive elements become polished. In the early stages of wear, tape movement becomes jerky and contact can be lost with the CTL/audio head (as in the case of the pressure roller), or the tape speed will become erratic (as in the case of the capstan belt). As the capstan pressure roller continues to wear the angle of the tape against the capstan shaft will change, causing the tape to ride up over the shaft, where it will be destroyed. (See Figure 7.12.)

ADJUSTING THE SERVO SYSTEMS

The replacement of a rubber component does

not always require an electronic adjustment. Those components responsible for mechanical drive, such as tape loading, do not; those that affect the precision drive of the tape, such as the capstan belt and pinch roller, do. Often, a recorder might exhibit a servo problem after a component has been replaced.

At first, all servo problems look the same— noise runs through the picture as the video heads run between the video tracks and the guard bands. A quick method for determining the difference between capstan motor problems and cylinder motor problems is to play back a "known" good tape, such as the standard alignment tape, while the recorder in the play STILL mode. In this mode, tape movement has been eliminated and therefore capstan servo operation. If the recorder reproduces a good, noise-free still picture, then the cylinder motor speed is consistent. Variations in cylinder servo speed will appear on the monitor as if someone is rotating the horizontal hold control. Once the tape is returned to the PLAY mode, if noise reappears in the picture and cannot be removed by adjustment of the tracking control, the problem is probably a capstan servo problem.

Replacement of rubber servo components usually has no effect on the cylinder servo because almost all recorders employ a direct-drive motor. However, due to the interaction between the servo systems, the repair or replacement of components on one servo will usually affect the other.

Servo Response Time

Changing servo rubber drive components has an effect of the response time of the servo system. The response time of a servo system determines the time required for the system to lock up to its incoming references. In general, servo lock-up time, from the point of greatest distortion (tape loading) will vary from three to five seconds, depending on the condition of the recorder. Lock-up time is much shorter for minor distortion (when the tape is running).

Response time is a function of the speed control, sometimes referred to as the discriminator control. To adjust the servo response time, compare the variable and fixed references and adjust the servo phase so the variable reference rides in the middle of the fixed reference. Create some distortion to the tape speed (capstan) or video head (cylinder), and observe how quickly the servo locks. Adjust the speed controls for the best response time. Adjust the cylinder servo first, then adjust the capstan servo.

CONCLUSION

In Part I of this book we have looked at the operation, maintenance and repair of videotape recorders. Part II focuses on the operation and repair of video cameras.

Part 2
Video Cameras

8 Viewing Color

HOW THE HUMAN EYE SEES COLOR

In viewing an object, the eye has the ability to reproduce images clearly over a wide range of lighting conditions. The ''perception'' of an object is dependent on its reflected light values. These values are a combination of the object's reflected luminance and the color of the light illuminating it.

Luminance

The luminance or light intensity of an object is perceived by the eye as brightness. Brightness is determined by the strength of the lighting source and the amount of light absorbed by the object—the eye sees the light that is reflected off the object. Luminance ranges from a value of 0% (black) to 100% (white); in between are the various shades of gray (see Figure 8.1). Starting from black and going towards white, each shade of gray absorbs less light and reflects more light towards the eye. If we start at white and move towards black, each step of gray absorbs more light and re-flects less light towards the eye. If we assume that we are dealing with absolutes at both ends of the scale, true gray would fall at the mid-point.

Chrominance

Chrominance is the addition of color to luminance. Color comes from both the lighting source and the light reflected by the object. Color values are described by hue and saturation.

Hue

Hue is the color itself. (Reds, blues and greens are hues.) Each color has a different wavelength within the visible spectrum of light, beginning with violet, which has the longest wavelength, and ending with red, which has the shortest wavelength. Each color within the spectrum absorbs a high degree of light, and therefore, has a low degree of reflectance, or relative brightness. Green, for example, is the brightest color because it exists in the middle of the spectrum and has the largest

91

Figure 8.1: Luminance values range from 0% (black) to 100% (white).

amount of reflected light. The three primary colors are positioned on the frequency spectrum as red, blue and green. White light is viewed as a mixture of 30% red, 11% blue and 59% green. As a result, most of what we see in white light is green and our eyes are most responsive to those objects that reflect green wavelengths.

Saturation

Saturation indicates the amount of white light that is mixed with a color—the greater the amount of white light, the more a color is diluted. The eye perceives these differences in color as "weak" or "strong," or as "purity." The greater the purity of a color, the less white light it contains.

Saturation is also defined by the reflectance of a color. At low light levels the eye is not able to "see" color. As the light falling on an object increases, not only can the eye see the color, but it can see the differences in the color.

The color of the lighting source adds to the color of the object—the resulting color is a product of both. For example, a white object illuminated by a red light takes on the tint of the red light, by reflecting it. The object seen by the eye, however, is not as *red* as the lighting source nor as *white* as the object itself—it sees a tint of red.

Color Temperature

The eye has two unique capabilities that enable it to see objects in varying light levels and lighting sources.

1. The eye can handle wide ranges of light. The iris opens and closes to adjust to different lighting conditions.
2. The eye retains the color consistency of an object under varying tristimistic (primary color temperature) lighting values.

Light differs not only in the amount of illumination it gives off, but also in its tristimistic value. Tristimistic values are measured in terms of color temperature. Color temperature is measured on the Kelvin scale, where 0° is an absolute value because it measures zero movement in the molecules of an object. From absolute zero colors are assigned temperature values as they emanate from burning carbon.

As coal burns, the color of its flame changes as the temperature increases. At a temperature of 3200° Kelvin, the light from burning carbon has a tristimistic brightness response similar to that of the human eye. Under this condition, blue equals 11%, red 30% and green 59%. The light given off by the burning coal is seen by the eye as white light. As the temperature of the flame increases, the percentage of each of the primary colors changes in relationship to the others. At 5500° Kelvin, red increases its share against green and blue, and the flame takes on a reddish hue. At the upper end of the color temperature scale, approximately 8000° Kelvin, the portion of blue increases, and the flame takes on a bluish hue.

The eye has the ability to compensate for such changes in the hue of an illumination source—a piece of white paper viewed under 3200° lighting would still appear as white when

Table 8.1: Color Filter Wheel Settings

Setting	Temperature Range	Primary Hue	Indoor Use	Outdoor Use
3200°K	2800°K to 4200°K	Red	Indoor: Used for initial camera setup and during studio production. The use of halogen-tungsten lighting emits a high degree of red.	Outdoor: Used during sunrise and sunset.
4500°K	4500°K to 5500°K	Red/Blue	Indoor: When using fluorescent lights.	Outdoor: Before and after the hours of 10 a.m. and 3 p.m., early morning and late afternoon.
5600°K	5600°K to 6000°K	Blue		Outdoor: Mid-afternoon sunlight. May also contain a neutral density filter to help reduce the amount of incoming light.
7000°K	7000°K to 8000°K	Blue		Outdoor: When shooting on cloudy or rainy days, or when shooting in the shade.

NOTE: K = Kelvin.

Table 8.2: Illumination Chart

Footcandles	Lux	Light Source
50	500	Office with multiple fluorescent lights.
100	1000	Clear sky during sunrise and sunset.
200	2000	Cloudy sky after sunrise and prior to sunset. TV studio lighting.
600	6000	Cloudy sky during midday.
9000	90,000	Clear sky during midday. (Neutral density filter required.)

viewed under 8000° Kelvin lighting. This, however, is not true of camera operation.

THE IMAGE PICKUP TUBE

Camera Chrominance

Image pickup devices do not have the ability to compensate for changes in color temperature as does the eye. Video cameras are preset at the factory to exhibit a consistent color reading under a color temperature of 3200° Kelvin, (the temperature emitted by halogen lighting; also called Quartz Iodine lighting). This type of lighting is used as a standard because its characteristics are closest to that of white light. A camera that has been properly set up will see a white object as white under these lights. Move the same camera outdoors, or change the lighting, and the white object will take on the prevailing color of the new lighting source. For example, as color temperature increases, so does its blue content. A white piece of paper viewed outdoors on a cloudy day when the prevailing light is blue would appear blue to a color camera.

In order for a color camera to correctly reproduce color, it is necessary that color temperature remain constant over varying light conditions. Of course, this is impossible to do by natural means alone. Cameras therefore use either an optical and/or electronic method to cause the image pickup tube to believe that it is seeing an object under 3200° Kelvin lighting conditions. Most ''industrial grade'' single-tube cameras and all three-tube cameras use optical color filter wheels located in front of the pickup tube. The filter system usually has a number of filters for the conversion process and one setting to completely block all light transmissions to the tube when the camera is not in use.

Table 8.1 contains typical settings for the camera color filter wheel, temperature range, primary hue and conditions for use.

After the color conversion wheel has been positioned, electronics are used to complete the color balance process. With the advent of microprocessor technology, electronic color balance can be achieved with the touch of a single button. Low-cost cameras, and those in the ''consumer'' range, limit color conversion to the electronic process only. In some cases (depending on the type of lens used) it is possible to place a color conversion filter on the front of the lens itself.

The best way to achieve good results is to plan ahead. Make sure that lighting conditions meet or exceed the camera's reference requirements. Avoid mixing different color temperature sources. For example, shooting next to a window will cause a mixture of indoor light (reddish) and outdoor light (bluish) making an accurate white balance adjustment extremely difficult. Likewise, all artificial light sources should have the same color temperature.

Camera Luminance: The Amount of Detail

Luminance is the amount of light the camera needs to ''see.'' Because luminance is tied to contrast, it plays a part in how well the details of an object are seen. Each color camera has different minimum and operational illumination requirements.

Footcandles

Specifications for camera performance or ''sensitivity'' center around the light level and camera lens f-stop that are used during camera setup. Light levels are measured in terms of ''footcandles'' (FC), which are units of illumination measured on a surface that is one foot from the light of one candle. Light can be rated in footcandle units, or lux, which is the unit for illumination used in international standards. A quick conversion from footcandles to lux is to multiply the number of footcandles by ten.

Cameras operating at light levels near or below the minimum requirement usually have a difficult time producing quality color pictures. Cameras operating in extremely high levels, such as more than 6000 footcandles, require the use of neutral density filters. Table 8.2 shows some typical footcandle and lux values for various shooting conditions.

CONCLUSION

The reproduction of color images by video cameras is a highly technical process. In this chapter we looked at the components of light and how they are viewed by the eye and camera pickup devices. In Chapter 9, we will review how color cameras create color.

9 How Color Cameras Create Color

THE THREE-TUBE COLOR CAMERA

Color cameras reproduce color by a process of color addition. By mixing the three primary colors—red, blue and green—at various levels of brightness, the color camera can produce secondary colors such as yellow, magenta and cyan. Yellow is formed by the combination of red and green; cyan is produced by mixing blue and green; and magenta is a combination of red and blue.

The process begins when light, received by the camera lens, is transmitted through a color conversion filter (which is responsible for maintaining a constant 3200° K temperature). Next, the light passes through a first-stage relay lens. Depending on the structure of the camera, the relay lens may also act as an infrared (IR) cut filter. (See Chapters 10 and 11, on image pickup devices, for a detailed discussion of infrared light.) The IR cut filter makes sure that the infrared light does not reach the pickup tube's faceplate. From this point, the remaining light is passed through a series of dichroic filters (prisms or mirrors) that focus an indi-

vidual primary color on the target of an individual tube. (See Figure 9.1.) In other words, the green filter allows only wavelengths in the green spectrum to be received and blocks transmissions of blue and red. When viewing a scene containing the three primary colors, the characteristics of the filtering system yield equal values of red, green and blue light. This is the equivalent of the camera seeing an object as white.

Dichroic Filters

Dichroic filters can be structured as mirror systems or prismatic systems.

Prism Systems

The first generation of studio cameras used the prismatic system, which positions the pickup tubes so that light is received through the least amount of lens relay—called the bayonet configuration. Since each of the tubes is positioned differently, the camera head had to be large. It became impossible to cost-effec-

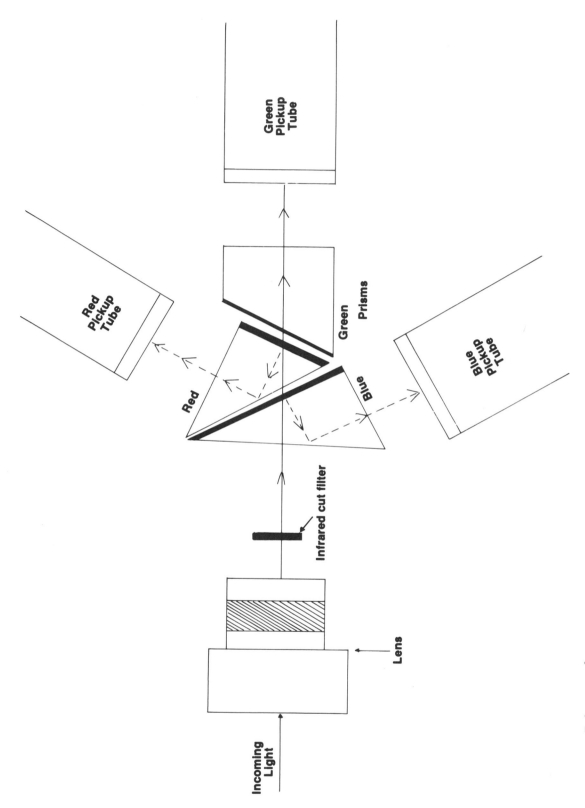

Figure 9.1: Prism optics.

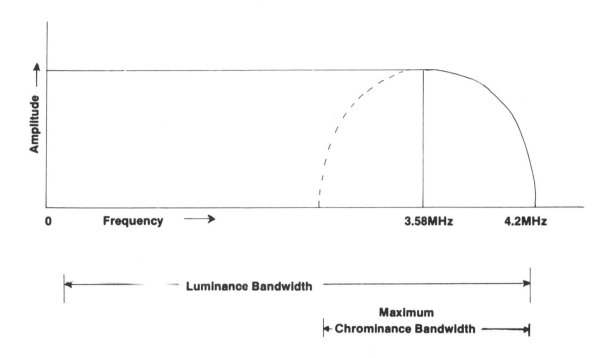

Figure 9.2: Comparison of luminance and chrominance bandwidths.

tively transfer prism optic technology into the early designs of ENG cameras. The scaling down of the optical block restricted prism optics to all but the high-end of "broadcast" cameras. The need for reasonably priced "industrial" cameras led to the development of the dichroic mirror system.

Mirror Systems

Mirror systems include an additional set of mirrors added to the relay lens that enable the pickup tubes to be arranged in parallel positions. This not only saves space, but also permits the use of a standard C Mount lens, as opposed to the bayonet configuration required by the prism optic systems. The advantages of lower costs and greater interchangeability of lenses had one major disadvantage, however. The addition of the mirrors to the prism resulted in only one half the amount of light reaching

the tube's target. Dichroic mirror cameras have to be operated at a lower number f-stop opening to equal the sensitivity of dichroic prism cameras.

Under low light conditions, prism optics yield better results, and although they are more expensive than mirror optics, recent advances in optical block construction and tube size have enabled prism optics to become a standard for some industrial cameras.

Matrixing the Color Signal

After the individual primary colors are received by the pickup tubes, they are fed to various processing circuits and combined to produce the output video signal. The combination of individual color channel outputs is done by the matrix circuits, which yield three types of signals—one luminance and two chrominance. The luminance channel is referred to as the Y channel, and contains all the primary colors proportioned to achieve white balance. The two chrominance channels provide all the color information in terms of hue and saturation. If we were dealing only with a closed circuit television system, we could use just the red, green and blue outputs (RGB output) without going through a matrix stage. These systems yield the greatest amount of resolution. However, most monitors and television sets are designed to see either a combined luminance/chrominance output or an RF signal. Color matrix systems were designed around RF transmissions, which are based on positioning a 3.58 MHz subcarrier within a 6 MHz channel bandwidth. All picture details are found within the luminance signal which ranges from 0 MHz to 4.2 MHz. (See Figure 9.2.) Color information is restricted to a narrower bandwidth of only ± 500 Hz, so it will not interfere with luminance and sound information. The greatest limitation to perceiving details within a color signal comes not from the television system, but from the human eye. Our eyes can perceive small details only in terms of brightness, void of the color qualities of hue and saturation. For example, if you look at the spans of a bridge at a distance, they appear to be either dark or light. However, as you move closer to the bridge, the spans begin to take on their color. It is hard for the eye to see color in objects that take up only a small area of the field of view.

Perceiving Secondary Colors

If we project a green light and blue light of equal brightness on a screen, and then combine the lights to produce cyan, the resulting secondary color contains less brightness than either of the original primary colors. This loss of brightness, which can also be expressed as a loss of resolution, gave rise to the Y, I and Q television encoding system. Y represents the luminance signal. The Q signal represents green and its bandwidth is limited to 0.5 MHz. The I signal, whose axis is 90° out of phase with the signal, contains a bandwidth of 1.5 MHz. The bandwidth of the I signal is increased as it vectorally represents either orange

(+I) or cyan (−I) which are the best hues for showing small details of color objects. Because of the requirements of the Y, I and Q signals, and the increase of the I signal bandwidth, details corresponding to 1/150 of the picture width can be seen. Color details contained within a 0.5 MHz signal, such as those contained in the Q signal, cannot be viewed past 1/25 of the total picture width.

It is important to recognize the role of the television monitor and receiver in perceiving the details in color pictures. All but the most expensive monitors, and all color television sets, receive color as R-Y and B-Y signals. Y represents all the primary colors in proportions of 0.30(R) + 0.59(G) + 0.11(B), so that R-(Y) and B-(Y) contain all the information needed to create the complete range of primary and secondary colors. This form of color matrixing limits the overall chroma bandwidth to 0.5 MHz, and is less complicated and expensive to produce. Since the monitor or television set is the final point for viewing the camera's output, using values of Y, I and Q, instead of R-Y and B-Y matrixing, is questionable in light of the method of demodulation used.

SINGLE-TUBE COLOR CAMERAS

The single-tube color camera is one of the greatest advances in the field of television. Not only did it significantly reduce the size and weight of the color camera, but for the first time, the reduction in cost put a color camera within the reach of the consumer.

Prior attempts to create a scaled down three-tube color camera led to the development of the two-tube camera, which combined the luminance and green signals on one tube, and the red and blue signals on the other. These cameras did not meet the requirements for small size and low cost.

The Stripe Filter System

To understand how the single-tube camera operates, we must first recognize that the pick-

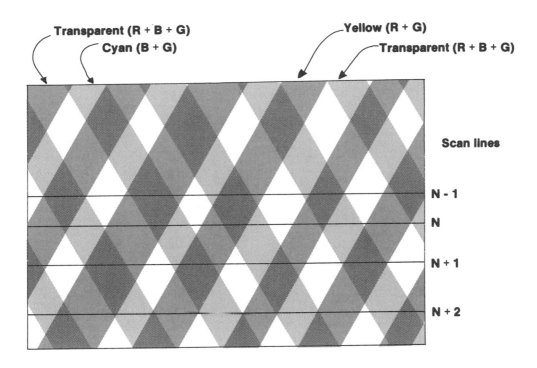

Figure 9.3: Stripe filter construction illustrating (N−1=N+1=N+3=N+5) and N=N+2=N+4) scanning.

up tube is "blind." As such, the process of creating red, blue and green signals must be done by some external component. This is the function of the stripe filter, which extracts the red, green and blue frequencies from the incident light. The stripe filter system is primarily a series of dichroic lenses, similar to those found in the optics of the three-tube color camera. (See Figure 9.3.) After passing through the optical stripe, the signal can be electronically separated into the red, green and blue primary colors, and processed in the same method used for three-tube cameras.

To understand the operation of the optical stripe filter system, we must first understand the concept of opposing hues.

Opposing Hues

When the primary colors red, green and blue are combined, they produce the range of secondary colors—cyan, magenta and yellow. When the primary colors are at unity, the result is white. When we begin to combine the primary colors, we can see that if we start with a greenish-yellow color, and add red, the yellow component decreases to the point where it equals green. The equal amounts of red and green create yellow. If we keep adding red, the color will become a yellowish red. No trace of redness appears until after the green component has disappeared. Likewise, if blue is added to greenish-yellow, the yellow component disappears first, leaving green and then bluish-green. Again, no blue appears until the yellow is cancelled. This relationship can be seen more clearly by looking at a Color Comp Graph. Colors positioned opposite from each other can be used as filters to block each other. This is the principle behind the dichroic stripes that are used to rate each of the primary colors of the single-tube color camera. For example,

YELLOW FILTER

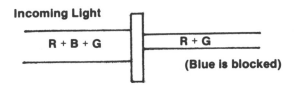

CYAN FILTER

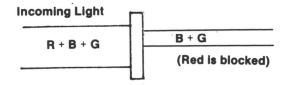

Figure 9.4: Color properties of yellow and cyan filters.

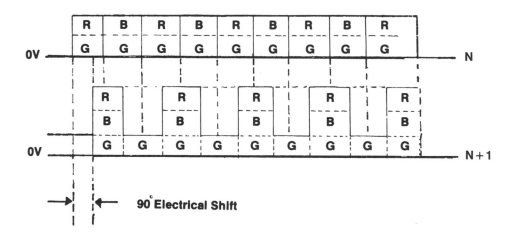

Figure 9.5: Dichroic stripe passing and blocking colors for scan lines N and N+1.

let's start with white light containing the three primary colors. If we pass the light through clear glass, the light maintains all its color content. When we place a yellow filter in front of the clear glass, only the red and green frequencies are passed—the blue light is blocked. If we replace the yellow filter with cyan colored glass, the red frequencies are blocked, and the blue and green frequencies are passed (see Figure 9.4).

By striping the faceplate of the pickup tube with dichroic filters, we can create an optical encoder. The stripes are set parallel to the vertical axis, and are scanned by the horizontal movement of the beam. If both the dichroic stripes are the same width, then as a result of the horizontal scan, they will be modulated at the same frequency. This would present a problem, as it would be impossible for the electronics to determine which frequency was a result of the cyan filter and which was a result of the yellow filter. To prevent this condition, the cyan and yellow stripes are positioned at different angles to the vertical plane. This has two advantages: First, at some point, both filters will cross each other. The combination of the cyan and yellow filters blocks both red and blue frequencies, allowing only green to pass. Second, the physical positioning of the stripes at different angles results in a frequency offset between the outputs of the cyan and yellow frequencies.

We will assume that our single-tube color camera contains a left running yellow stripe and a right running cyan stripe. Both stripes are positioned at a 25° angle from the vertical axis.[1]

Further, each dichroic stripe is separated by a clear or transparent stripe. We can pick any point on the active horizontal scan and determine what color or colors are blocked or passed. For example, let's follow the path of scan line "N." It begins by passing through the yellow filter, which yields a red and green (yellow) signal. (See Figure 9.5.) Next, it passes through the cyan filter, producing a blue-green (cyan) signal. This pattern continues for the rest of this horizontal scan line. On the next horizontal line (N + 1) the beam passes through alternating clear glass,

passing red, green and blue, and the combined cyan and blue filters, which only passes green. As you can see, the green frequency serves as the carrier for the red and blue components.

Now let's look at lines N and N + 1 in terms of their color output. The physical offset results in a 90° phase difference between the peaks of the blue and red signals. This offset can be used to separate the common frequency into these individual colors. By positioning this specific chroma carrier frequency above the wider band of the green carrier, we can separate the two groups by using a lowpass filter (green) and a bandpass filter (red, blue.) In addition, the bandwidth of the green signal allows it to contain the luminance (detail) information.

Now that we have optically encoded the colors, we have to decode them into separate red and blue signals. By using the successive phase shifted lines, the chroma carrier can be divided into two paths. One is shifted an additional 90° and the other is delayed by one horizontal line. The additional phase shift, 1-H delay, and inversion technique is used to obtain red signals through an additive process, and blue through a subtractive process.

Remember that the optical system physically created a 90° difference between the red and blue frequencies. When we add an additional 90° phase shift, the difference will be 180°. By dividing the carrier into two paths, and sending one through a 1-H delay line, we achieve the following: Adding lines 1 and 2 will yield a doubled red signal and zero blue output. Subtracting lines 1 and 2 will yield a zero red output and a blue output. (See Figure 9.6.)

At this point, we have all the elements needed to produce an encoded color output signal that is viewable on a monitor. The Y luminance signals provide the details as well as the element for R-Y, B-Y encoding.

SINGLE-TUBE COLOR CAMERA PROBLEMS

Problems with single-tube color cameras occur when the subject matter cannot meet the minimum operating conditions of the optical stripe. The first drawback is usually the light

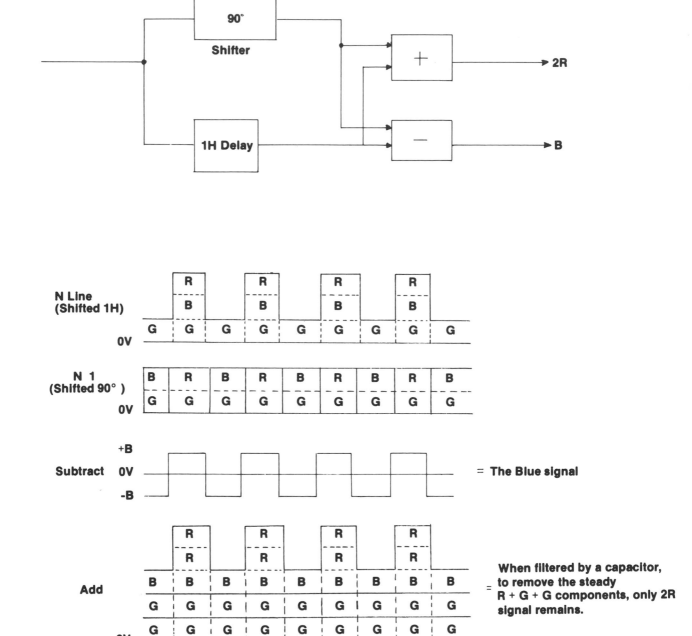

Figure 9.6: Red and blue signals extracted with a stripe filter.

requirement. All color reproduced by the single-tube camera is dependent upon the ability of the tube to see the dichroic stripe filter. When light conditions are too low, the details of the stripe are lost. When light conditions are too high, the beam saturates due to excessive beam transmissions, and the stripe is washed out. In either case, the loss of the stripe means red and blue cannot be produced. The resulting output of the system is the carrier frequency—green. In order to avoid this condition, most single-tube color cameras contain a chroma chip circuit that eliminates any chroma information under extremely low and high light conditions.

The second problem encountered with single-tube color cameras involves the shape of the object being viewed. Sharp contrasts result in the creation of high-frequency transitions on the target faceplate. When these frequencies approach the frequency of the stripe filter, the camera will interpret them as color information generated by the dichroic filter. To avoid this condition, high-frequency luminance signals must be attenuated. A simple, but unacceptable method would be to defocus the lens. Another, better method is to place a lens in front of the target that will roll off high frequencies without affecting the transitions created by the dichroic filter.

Overall resolution is another drawback of the single-tube color camera. In the frequency modulated system, luminance cannot exceed the color carrier, because it would result in interference between the two. One solution is to raise the frequency of the color carrier. This is easier said than done. The carrier frequency is comprised of a complex relationship that can be expressed by the following equation:

$$F = W(mm)/P(um) \times T(us) \times 10 \text{ to the third power (MHz)}$$

Where:

F = The color carrier frequency, expressed in MHz.

P = Dichroic stripe pitch expressed in micrometers.

W = Effective horizontal scanning width of the pickup tube, expressed in millimeters.

T = Effective horizontal scanning period of the pickup tube expressed in microseconds.

By increasing the horizontal scanning width and lowering the pitch, higher carrier frequencies can be achieved. Frequency modulated stripe filter systems have seen carrier increases from 3.6 MHz in first generation cameras introduced in 1973, to 4.3-MHz carriers found in today's "high band" tubes. This increase in carrier frequency has yielded an effective increase in luminance resolution from approximately 250 horizontal lines to 300 horizontal lines.

---

[1]NOTE: The actual angle between the dichroic filters and the vertical axis is determined by the following formula: Phase angle = arctan 1.55 f, where f equals the modulating frequency of the carriers in MHz.

10 Image Pickup Devices: Tubes

The most basic component of any color camera is its image pickup device. The majority of cameras today use tubes. In this chapter we will look at image pickup tubes, how they operate and the different types available. (Figure 10.1 illustrates the typical image pickup tube.) Solid state or image pickup devices that use integrated circuits are discussed in Chapter 11.

HOW PICKUP TUBES WORK

The eyes of the pickup tube are contained on the photoconductive surface that forms a mosaic on the tube's glass faceplate (see Figure 10.2). The photoconductive material, which is stored inside the tube, acts as a capacitor. Light creates areas of discharge that are focused on the tube's faceplate (see Figure 10.3). The greater the intensity of the light, the greater the number of discharges. The incoming light creates these discharges by releasing the electrons of the target faceplate, thereby upsetting its neutrality. Each spot on the target that has released electrons takes on a positive potential and looks for a source to replace its missing

electrons. That source is found in the cathode section of the tube. When the cathode is heated, it takes on a negative potential and becomes a source of electrons. With the target faceplate having a positive potential and the cathode having a negative potential, a flow of electrons from the cathode to the target is created. This electron flow is called the target current. The side of the faceplate that is directed toward the cathode is reduced to the same potential as the cathode by the electron beam. As a result, the target's positive potential increases.

The electron beam reads across the varying tube faceplate and deposits more charges on those sections of the tube with higher positive potentials. These sections of the target are receiving more incoming light. Fewer charges are deposited on the target sections that have less of a potential difference. These target sections receive less light. The signal across the total target faceplate is equal to the signal discharged by the incoming light. The video signal is created by the resistive load contained in the target circuit.

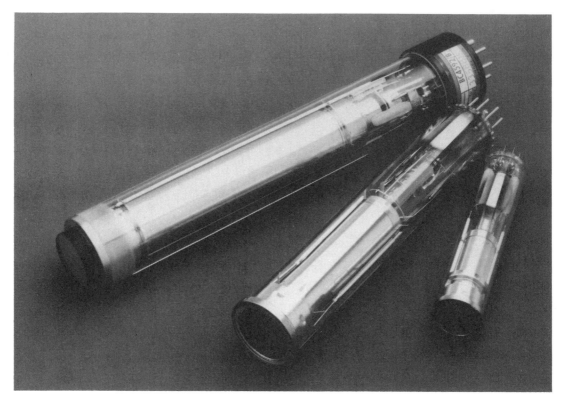

Figure 10.1: Camera pickup tubes. Photo courtesy of Amperex.

The transmission of electrons from the cathode to the target is aided by the use of an external electrical source, which applies voltage to the faceplate (target voltage) and the cathode (beam). Current flow is from the positive target to the negative cathode. A load resistor positioned between the target and cathode produces the output signal. Changing light levels on the faceplate generate changing current on the load resistor. As more light falls on the target, the signal output across the load increases. In the ideal situation, a tube would increase the light input and signal output in a linear proportion. However, tubes are not perfect, so neither are their light transfer capabilities. Light input can only increase to the point at which the faceplate begins to satu-

rate. At this point, the output falls off. This is known as the tube's *Gamma Characteristic*.

Gamma Characteristic

At the opposite end of the television system from the camera is the monitor. The monitor projects its picture by means of a cathode ray tube (CRT). The gamma characteristic of the CRT is created by the electron beam current and the picture tube phosphor output (or brightness). The processes of light falling on the pickup tube target and light emitted by the CRT are opposites, therefore, so are their gamma curves. However, though they are opposites they are not equal. The gamma exponent of a typical CRT lies between 2.0 and 2.2. To achieve a

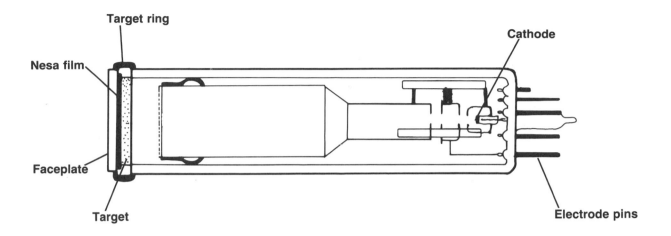

Figure 10.2: Construction of pickup tube.

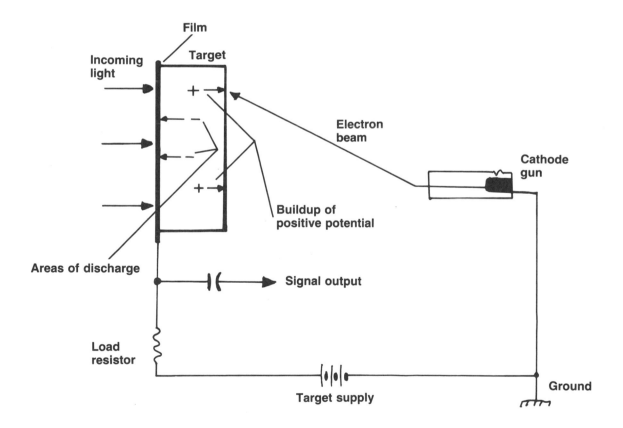

Figure 10.3: Signal circuit of the pickup tube as light hits the faceplate.

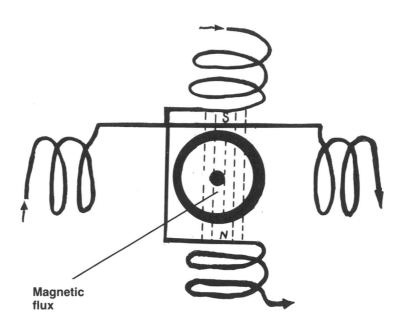

Magnetic
flux

Figure 10.4: Placement of deflection coils in yoke assembly.

linear gamma output, the camera tube should have a gamma range of 0.45 to 0.6. Gamma correction is done elctronically in the camera to achieve a uniform relationship between the camera light input and the tube output.

Tube Deflection

To create a picture that can be viewed by the television receiver, the horizontal and vertical deflection rates of the camera scanning beam must be exactly the same as those of the television monitor. The process of beam alignment begins with a series of magnets that are located in the deflection (or yoke) assembly of the camera. The pickup tube is clamped inside this yoke assembly. An auxiliary magnetic field is responsible for centering the beam within the tube. The beam must be properly focused if it is to land precisely in the center of the target. This can be accomplished in two ways. The first method of magnetic deflection uses deflection coils that are wound inside the deflection yoke (see Figure 10.4). The coils create a magnetic field that sets up a direct current to guide the beam.

The second method, called electrostatic focus, uses deflection grids that are located inside the tube. This method reduces total power consumption of the camera by eliminating the need to drive the external focus coils. It is primarily used for ENG and EFP applications.

After the beam has been emitted by the cathode, it is accelerated and passed through a limiting aperture. At this point, it is focused by the electron static grids. A final set of grids assure that the beam lands perpendicular to the target. Once the beam has properly landed on the faceplate, two sets of deflection coils, one set for vertical and another for horizontal, begin the scanning process.

DARK CURRENT

Light absorption on the target faceplate is an imperfect process, as is the transfer of electrons between the cathode and the target. Tube imperfections can vary and have significant affects on a camera's output picture and quality.

The incident light falling on the target increases the current across the target load resistor and increases signal output. Bright objects reflect large amounts of light and produce high signal outputs. Dark objects reflect less light and produce low tube currents. In the ideal pickup tube, if no light reached the pickup surface, the signal output would be zero, because there would be no current flow. The pickup tube, however, is part of an electronic circuit, and as long as power is supplied to the circuit, current flows. The least amount of current is present when the pickup tube sees the darkest portions of an object. Black, therefore, is represented by the lowest measure of current flow. When no incident light is present, the resulting beam current is the dark current. The higher the dark current, the "lighter" dark objects will appear. This low overall contrast range reduces picture details. In addition, the high amount of electron transmission adds noise to the dark areas, and lowers the overall signal-to-noise ratio.

Dark currents have a tendency to increase the longer a tube remains in constant operation, due to the internal heat that builds up because of cathode and heater current. Increases in temperature cause drops in internal resistance. If we assume that in most cases the target voltage will remain at its fixed setting, then the current must increase. It is therefore desirable to have a tube system that exhibits a stable dark current. The target should be set to the voltage specified in the camera's service manual. Settings lower than normal will affect overall sensitivity and dynamic range. Settings

that are too high will increase the speed at which the electrons hit the faceplate, to create a condition known as secondary emissions in which individual electrons strike the target surface more than once. This increase of beam current and secondary emissions can damage the target by punching holes through the faceplate structure.

THE ELECTRON BEAM

The beam flows constantly as long as power is applied to the tube. From a user viewpoint, the beam can be described as the amount of current that flows when the greatest amounts of incident light strike the faceplate. Unlike the dark current, the beam has no absolute value setting. Each tube should have the capability to discharge light levels that are a minimum of double its normal operation condition. For example, if a camera's specifications indicate that it has a normal sensitivity of 200 FC (footcandles) at a lens setting of f-4.0 (this setting, under the proper amount of light, will produce a video level output of 100 IRE, which is considered to be a full video signal output), then by changing the lens opening to f-2.8 and allowing double the amount of light to reach the tube, the resulting picture will resolve all picture details.

Due to its inability to anticipate contrast ratios (except under very controlled studio conditions), the beam must be discharged at a level at least twice its specified operating condition. If the beam is set lower than normal, blooming occurs (positive picture highlights become washed out) because the excess electrons have no place to go. Setting the beam higher than normal distorts the fidelity of picture reproduction, particularly in the corners. But the greatest problem is a shortening of tube life because of increases in the tube current.

Beam Misalignment

Problems encountered during the yoke and tube manufacturing processes can cause beam misalignment. When this occurs, the beam does not reach the physical center of the target, and the strike angle is altered from 90°. When viewing the picture from a tube with poor beam alignment, focus, particularly in the corner areas, looks soft and reproduced shapes do not conform to their original geometry. Beam misalignment in one tube of a three tube camera system can create registration problems because the lack of corner focus prevents exact overlapping of one tube's image with the others.

TUBE LAG

The tube's target faceplate is a mosaic of thousands of capacitive and resistive elements. The capacitor is formed between the front of the signal plate and its back surface, which receives electrons from the cathode. When the beam starts, it strikes the back surface of the faceplate and a difference in electronic potential is created. The target area contains resistive elements that are placed parallel to the target capacitors. These create the discharge path. The amount of resistance of this resistor/capacitor (RC) network is dependent upon the amount of incoming light that is striking the faceplate. The greater the amount of incident light, the lower the overall target resistance. The higher the overall target resistance, the lower the amount of incoming incident light.

Pickup tubes must be able to quickly adapt to change. Every 1/30th of a second a new picture is imposed on the tube's target. If a new scene changes the amount of light hitting the faceplate in any particular area, the electronic potential of that area also changes. For example, when a camera lens is capped, the transition time between the previous picture and the drop to dark current is usually within one frame. Lag is determined by measuring the amount of the previous picture that is still visible after the completion of the third scanning field. This entire process is usually completed within 50 milliseconds.

The RC Time Constant

The main factor contributing to lag is the RC time constant of the tube. The RC time constant is the term applied to a circuit in which a resistor (R) and capacitor (C) are together and the time it takes to charge or discharge the capacitor through the resistor. The value of the RC time constant is often determined by the material used to create the pickup target surface.

Resistance changes can also be affected by the beam transmissions. Beam velocities within the tube are low to begin with. As the beam reaches the target surface, its velocity is reduced to zero, or that of the cathode voltage, so that not all the electrons will reach the target surface at the same time. Due to these differences in electron velocity, an amount of time will pass before an equilibrium voltage is reached. It is during this time that lag is produced.

Beam alignment can also affect lag. While target capacitance is a fixed factor of target composition, beam resistance can be varied by changing beam alignment. Because the beam strikes the faceplate at zero velocity, the strike angle should present the least amount of resistance to beam landing. This occurs when the strike angle is 90°. Improper beam alignment increases the apparent target resistance, thereby increasing the RC time constant and lag.

TUBE RESOLUTION

Tube resolution is dependent on target, beam and alignment setups. In measuring a tube's resolution, what we really are determining is its ability to receive light and transfer the beam to the associated circuits to create the output signal. This transfer of light energy to signal output takes place on the target faceplate. Again, the determining factor is the composition of the target faceplate. In the ideal situation, the target would have an extremely large number of light absorbing particles, which would be scanned by a direct beam having a small diameter compared to the total scan of the faceplate. Such a tube would be quick to react to changes in incoming light to produce sharp contrasts and high degrees of picture resolution. Problems arising from high dark current affect picture contrast. Problems with misalignment of the beam affect output resolution.

Tubes with high dark currents and lag have lower resolution than low dark current, low lag tubes. Spectral response also plays a part in tube resolution. Tubes, like the human eye, are most responsive to the green component of light. As a result, light transfer and output resolution is greatest in light containing a high degree of green frequencies.

TYPES OF PICKUP TUBES

Nothing characterizes a camera better than its image pickup tube. The type of tube used not only determines performance, but also camera cost. Tubes differ primarily in the area of target composition. Selecting the correct camera is a matter of selecting the tube that meets your operating requirements. The three tubes we will be discussing in this section are the Vidicon, Plumbicon and Saticon tubes.

When color first appeared in broadcasting, the need for high performance demanded the use of the highest quality tube—the Plumbicon (Pbo, lead oxide). The cost of this tube precluded it from use for industrial (nonbroadcast) applications. As a result, camera manufacturers turned to the Vidicon tube. This tube actually preceded the Plumbicon tube by almost 10 years, but never developed into the type of tube that broadcasters deemed acceptable. The Saticon tube, which is similar to the Plumbicon tube in characteristics, was introduced to the video industry as a high performance tube developed at low cost.

The Vidicon Tube

Images are formed on the faceplate, which is sealed to the glass tube. The junction between the faceplate and the tube is covered by a target ring which serves as the conductive element for signal transmission. An electron conductive film—Nesa Film—(refer to Figure 10.2) is applied to the faceplate by spraying a tin chloride solution to the faceplate after it has been superheated. For the Vidicon tube, the Nesa film is lined with antimony trisulfide. The layer is approximately five microns thick and has a dark (no signal) resistance of (1×10^{12})

ohms per centimeter. Since images are created by the capacitive and resistive elements of the photoconductive film reacting to the intensity of the incoming light, the Nesa film is charged to the value of the target voltage through the load resistor. As the film is scanned by the negative beam, the gun side (inner side) is reduced to the cathode potential. This difference leaks across the resistance of the film producing the output signal.

The Vidicon tube is distinguished from other tubes by its varying target potential, which causes its sensitivity to vary. Normally, this sensitivity might be considered an advantage if the target material could rapidly discharge itself. This is not the case with the Vidicon, in which any increase in the target potential causes more electrons to strike the faceplate. During nontransmission or dark periods, the electrons are slowly bled off due to the bulk of the Vidicon's photoconductive layer. Under low light levels, the dark current is high, approximately 20 nanoamps (na) and the tube slowly gives up its previous image. As a result, the Vidicon tube has the greatest amount of lag time, the lowest signal-to-noise ratio and the lowest sensitivity. In addition, the high amounts of tube transmission under low light levels tend to reduce overall tube life.

The Plumbicon Tube

In the Plumbicon tube (Pbo), the Nesa film is lined with a lead oxide photoconductive film. As with the Vidicon tube, the film is applied by means of evaporation. The Pbo's film consists of three layers: Sb_2S_3, Pbo and SnO_2. The layer nearest the beam side contains the doped Pbo (doped refers to the addition of ions into a material). The SnO_2 plate is located at the front end of the tube. Both these layers are relatively thin, therefore, much of the thickness is contained in the middle layer. This structure is the key to Plumbicon operation. The negative beam strikes the layer nearest to it first, thereby charging it negative with respect to the layer on the window side. The target structure becomes reverse biased, resulting in low conductivity. With the absence of light, only a small amount of dark current flows.

Due to the structure of the target, a gap is present between the lead oxide and outer layers. Even in the presence of higher ambient temperatures, which are found after tubes warm up, the dark current still remains as low as 0.3 na. In the Plumbicon tube, lag is the lowest found in any image pickup tube and signal-to-noise ratio is the highest.

The Saticon Tube

The target of the Saticon tube is a combination of selenium, arsenic and tellurium. The name Saticon is derived from Se-As-Te Chalcongenide glass. As opposed to the Pbo tube, the target of the Saticon tube is a combination of many layers that produce a high degree of storage capacitance. Uncorrected, the amount of lag developed in the element junction would make the tube unusable in all but high uniform light situations. To correct this condition, light emitting diodes are positioned to provide uniform illumination to the target. "Bias light," as it is called, corrects for excessive lag by bringing the dark current up to that of a low light level video signal. At this low signal level, the electrons landing on the faceplate cause it to go negative compared to the target. This continuous even flow of electrons reduces lag. In addition, bias light provides an extremely stable reference black for the camera system.

TUBE PERFORMANCE

The truest test of any camera (or camera tube) is its output picture quality. What we see as its output is a function of resolution and color reproduction.

Spectral Response of the Vidicon Tube

Each tube has its own spectral response. Within this range of light frequencies, resolution is maximum. Due to the amount of signal amplification needed for each tube's particular

range of color, spectrum response is less than for the other primary colors. For example, the spectrum response of a Vidicon tube peaking in the 500 to 600 nanometer range contains the green frequencies. While resolution response within the green frequency range is good, response in the blue and red ranges falls off compared to the green, and details from blue and red objects are poor. The photoconductive material of the Vidicon target will reflect or absorb light based on its frequency. While blue frequencies are absorbed, red light bounces around the target junction and is eventually reflected into its backside. This causes red objects to look soft.

Due to its spectrum sensitivity, the camera electronics need to work harder to bring the blue and red levels up to that of the green to produce an acceptable white balance. This process of amplifying low level signals usually adds noise that compounds with the noise produced by the Vidicon's high dark current transmissions. As a result, signals produced from a single tube Vidicon color camera will tend to be noisy and low in resolution in all except well lit locations.

Spectral Response of the Plumbicon Tube

In general, the spectrum response of a Pbo tube mirrors the human eye closer than any other tube. Like the eye, it lacks responses in the infrared (IR) regions. While this is an advantage, it is also a major disadvantage. The overall thickness of the Pbo target layer will determine its response to a particular spectrum region. A thin layer response is better to blue than to red. It follows, therefore, that tubes must be individually selected according to their responses to a particular spectrum of light. The sensitivity, lag, image retention and even the number of tube spots of a Pbo depend on the frequency of light it is viewing. In order to maximize the performance of the Pbo camera, each tube must be selected to match a particular color channel; red, green or blue. Replacement tubes must be ordered according to the individual channel that requires replacement. Even this process of individual tube selection does not solve all the problems of Pbo camera performance. The average thickness layer of the Plumbicon target will have a positive effect on red resolution. This is due to the movement of electrons within the target layers. The ideal compromise would be a thinner layer, which maintains an acceptable absorption level for red frequencies. The "extended red" Pbo tube accomplishes just that. Sensitivity in the red region is almost double that of a normal red Pbo tube, while resolution is increased approximately 30%. All this good is not possible without some trade offs, however. Burn in and lag time are increased due to the increase in target absorption. This can result in increased red highlighting or tube flaring. Cameras using extended red tubes require additional red compensation circuits, which electronically try to surpass this condition.

Spectral Response of the Saticon Tube

When compared to the Pbo tube, the spectral response of the Saticon is very close, even when we are taking the extended red tube into consideration. Unlike the Pbo, light is absorbed directly into the faceplate of the Saticon tube, and little is reflected back into the tube itself. As a result, little flare is created during high contrast shooting. By separating the target photoconductor from the inner tube atmosphere and adding arsenic doping to prevent target crystallization, tube life is increased and surface blemishes decrease.

NEW TUBE DEVELOPMENT

Amperex

Tube development did not stop with the introduction of the Saticon tube. Broadcasters required further reduction in lag time and increases in resolution and signal-to-noise ratios. Resolution and lag are related to each other through the action of the tube's photoconduc-

tive target. As lag is reduced, the beam can respond more quickly to changes in contrast, which results in greater definition between the dark and light areas of a reproduced object. This definition can be maintained until the frequencies, or rate of transitions, become too great for the camera system to handle. At this point, the camera system will begin to surpress the amplitude of these higher frequencies, a condition called depth of modulation. Although the Pbo provided the best color reproduction, the Saticon offered similar color response with a greater depth of modulation. In response to the performance of the Saticon, Amperex, the manufacturer of the Plumbicon tube, began working on increasing the depth of modulation of the Pbo tube by reducing its photoconductive layer. By decreasing lag, the resolution response is increased, since both factors are dependent on the amount of time it takes the tube's signal current to change. This time factor can be expressed by the formula:

$$T = RC, \text{ where}$$

- T = time for a change to occur.
- R = beam resistance, which is determined by the velocity spread of the electron beam.
- C = faceplate capacitance, which is determined by faceplate thickness.

From this formula, we can clearly see that by decreasing the value of R or C or both, the value of T (lag) will be reduced. As the target of any tube is capacitive, researchers found that they could lower overall tube capacity by increasing the size of the photoconductive layers. This is the equivalent of adding more capacitors in series, which has the effect of reducing the total amount of capacity.

The Diode Gun Tube

With the problem of faceplate capacity solved, researchers began to work on the possibility of reducing beam resistance. In the structure of the diode gun tube, grid one is made positive with respect to the cathode. This diode configuration increases beam acceleration and results in less beam spread and lower beam resistance. By lowering both beam resistance and faceplate capacitance, less lag and greater depth of modulation were achieved. In order to achieve greater signal-to-noise ratio, researchers looked outside the tube.

Since the image pickup tube is basically noise free, system noise is a function of the input FET (Field Effect Transistor) amplifier and the load resistor shunted by the tube's internal capacitance. Load resistance is usually a fixed factor, not subject to change. This leaves the FET and tube capacity. Advances in FET technology decresed input capacity. In order to decrease tube-to-yoke capacity, a target contact was added to the faceplate. This process eliminated the need for a target ring and its associated shunt capacitance. As a result, more signal containing higher frequencies and less noise is transferred to the first stage pre-amplifier. (Although Amperex started research on this technology in 1969, it was not until the early 1980s that the Low Output Capacitance Tube—LOC Tube—was made available.)

Hitachi

Like Amperex, Hitachi, manufacturer of the Saticon tube, added a direct target contact pin to the faceplate of its tube to reduce shunt capacity. In addition, diode gun Saticons also appeared. Like their Pbo counterparts, the Saticon diode gun tubes contained an immediate positive grid to further narrow beam deflection and increase resolution.

Although bias light solved the major lag problem of the Saticon tube, it did so by external means. The basic structure of the Saticon caused an undesirable effect when it was operated under extreme contrast conditions. For example, if an ENG Saticon camera was used to shoot a fire, the extreme contrast and heat caused by the fire would result in a comet tail effect similar to that of the Plumbicon tube. Prolonged exposure caused the image to permanently burn into the faceplate of the Saticon. ENG news crews covering fires quickly learned about this drawback. Recent Saticon developments have centered around the addition of doping elements to the target. These developments lead to the introduction of the RCA and Hitachi Saticon 2 and Saticon 3 tubes, which claim to reduce image burn and lag by 75%.

MEASURING TUBE GRADE AND QUALITY

Each manufacturer rates the acceptability of its tubes by measuring the flaws and spots on the target faceplates. Spots are caused by impurities which occur during the manufacturing process. In some cases, due to these impurities, a manufacturer may offer various "grades" of tubes. Amperex classifies its Plumbicons into "industrial" and "broadcast" grades. The grade is determined by the outcome of a "Spurious Signals Test." This test fixes the number of permissible flaws according to an established tube zone. Although levels of acceptability vary from manufacturer to manufacturer, the method for measuring flaws is standard. The target faceplate is divided into three zones: Zone 1, Zone 2 and Zone 3. An individual spot is determined by its average contrast range compared to the white level. A white spot is any flaw whose signal output exceeds 40% of the white level (100% IRE). A black spot is any flaw that has a video output of 50% below the average white level.

CONCLUSION

Vidicon tubes offer the lowest cost and performance specifications. Usually, a Vidicon camera is configured as a single tube color camera. Plumbicon tubes, on the other hand, have limitations such as individual color selectivity, which make them unsuitable for configurations other than in a three tube camera. This is where the Saticon tube demonstrates its versatility. Due to its wide spectral response, it can be configured in either a single tube or three tube color camera.

Our discussion has been limited to the major types of tubes found in today's color cameras. There are many other types of tubes, such as the Visticon (RCA), Chicon (Toshiba) and Newvicon (Panasonic). Like Plumbicons, Visticons and Chicons are usually used in three tube cameras. Newvicons are found in single tube cameras, where they provide better dark current and burn resistance than Vidicon tubes.

Recent camera developments have also seen the introduction of integrated circuit "chip" image pickup devices. Chip cameras are discussed in Chapter 11.

11 Image Pickup Devices: Chips

Chip cameras represent one of the most dramatic changes in the broadcast industry since the introduction of the Plumbicon tube. First introduced in the early 1970s, these devices have had limited application because of their high cost and low quality signal outputs. Current solid state image pickup devices are either charge coupled devices (CCD) or metal oxide semiconductor (MOS). MOS technology preceded CCD by approximately four years, but limitations in resolution and dynamic range prevented its use as a suitable replacement for the image pickup tube.

CCD offers the capability of imaging objects over a wide range of lighting conditions. Both types of chips offer dramatic improvements over the conventional pickup tube. And, chip cameras have proven to be more rugged, lighter in weight, lower in power consumption and require little or no setup—features that are extremely important for ENG/EFP applications.

Lower power consumption means that the camera/videotape recorder combination can operate for longer periods of time without requiring a battery change. Less complex setup makes for easier and more exact setup under difficult circumstances, or when the camera is operated by inexperienced personnel.

Since both CCD and MOS cameras are comprised of integrated circuits, their differences in performance and problems relating to their signal outputs are the results of the different methods used to project images on the chip and the methods used to output the resulting signal.

PRINCIPLES OF MOS OPERATION

The single picture element of a MOS pickup device contains a photosensitive section that is made up of many individual metal oxide semiconductors. Within the silicon material area (the potential well) a junction photodiode is created when a pair of closely spaced polysilicon electrodes are placed on the surface. If the voltage of the MOS switch is alternately raised and lowered, the electrons will move. When the switch is off, incident incoming light creates subcarriers that are collected in the polysilicon junction. (See Figure 11.1.)

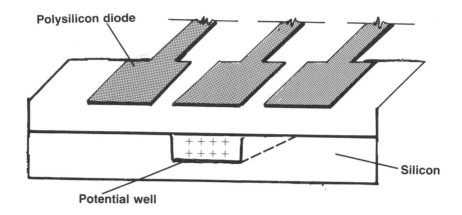

Figure 11.1: Schematic of MOS pickup device.

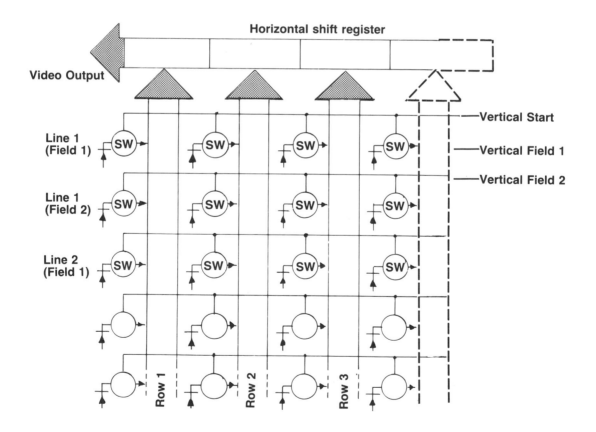

Figure 11.2: Interline transfer.

The amount of incoming light is limited by the voltage that reverse biases the polysilicon diode. This is called the video voltage. When the MOS switch turns on, the charged voltage is read out by the scanning circuits, which shift the signals off each element sequentially through an analog switch onto a common vertical bus. The horizontal switches are turned on in time sequence by the output pulses of the horizontal shift register. The resulting charge that is read out of each element creates a signal that is proportional to the amount of incoming light.

By using both horizontal and vertical shift registers (interline transfer), compatibility with the NTSC system can be maintained. (See Figure 11.2.)

PRINCIPLES OF CCD OPERATION

CCD is an analog signal created by closely spaced groupings, called arrays. As in a pickup tube, incoming light causes a change in the electronic potential of the pickup tube surface. In the case of the CCD, incident light generates minority carriers (electrons) in the silicon. The more incoming light there is, the greater the amount of electrons generated. By grouping CCDs in arrays and focusing light on the arrays via a lens, the potential at any given point on the array will be the result of the amount of incident light received. In order for the signal to maintain compatibility with NTSC standards, the image is transferred to a storage area during vertical blanking and read out of the storage area at the horizontal rate. Little energy is lost during the transfer process, so efficiency can be as high as 99%.

DIFFERENCES BETWEEN CCD AND MOS DEVICES

Even though MOS and CCD devices appear to be similar, their performances are quite different.

In CCD devices, the signal is held in a junction beneath the MOS capacitor. Readout is then accomplished by multiple transfers. In MOS devices, the signal charge is held in a photodiode. Readout is done by a single transfer. Although these differences might seem minor, they produce great differences at light level extremes. At low light levels, the ability to resolve a picture will depend on the efficiency of the sensor to collect incident light and transfer it to a signal. MOS devices transfer light more efficiently than CCD devices.

Under high light conditions, the concern is saturation exposure. This parameter is a function of the maximum charge obtained during the light gathering period. The time required for the photo elements to gather charges is approximately equal to the time it takes to record one frame of video. High light capability can be maximized by increasing the storage capacity of the individual regions of the photo elements. MOS benefits most from this technique because information in the photo element must be read out. Longer transfer times and lower transfer efficiency caused by multiple transfers result in blurred images.

The greatest problem for both types of chip image devices is transfer noise, which limits the overall signal-to-noise ratio of the camera. This noise is caused by the use of capacitance to transfer signals. In MOS devices, noise is generated from a fixed noise pattern (FNP), which appears in the form of spikes occurring at the vertical rate as the switching transfer transistors are turned on and off. The spikes are generated at twice the highest frequency. At the vertical rate, smear can occur due to leak through of the photogenerated electrons to the vertical signal line. Under high light conditions, the chip can create a vertical white stripe extending from the upper and lower edges of the picture highlight area. Although CCDs also generate FPN due to the capacitance between clock output lines, this type of FPN is low in frequency compared to the output video and as such, can be eliminated by the use of a low pass filter. The major problem with CCDs is limitation of dynamic range. Under high light (high contrast) conditions, the slowness of signal transfer limits the amount of signal that the CCD can handle. If the larger amounts (high levels) of signal cannot be transferred out of the cell in a timely manner, the cell will oversaturate, causing blooming. To solve the problem, the CCD cell requires the use of an overflow drain. While this method effectively handles the blooming problem, the loss of cell real estate reduces the photosensitivity, decreasing dynamic range.

Solving Oversaturation

The drawbacks in both MOS and CCD devices would render them unacceptable for use in television cameras if it were not for advances in the field of MOS technology.

MOS FPN at the horizontal rate can be cancelled through a process of interratation. The vertical rate smear problem is suppressed by an external circuit, which uses an analog-to-digital converter that holds the smear element in memory and reads it out during the vertical blanking period. By subtracting the stored smear component from the signal at each point of a picture, the vertical smear can be suppressed to very low levels under normal exposure conditions.

The blooming problem can be handled by reading out the overflow during the picture's vertical interval into a vertical overflow drain (VOD), which is positioned under the photo sensor material. As a result, the overflow problem is solved without sacrificing the photoelectronic pickup area.

CHIP CAMERA CONSTRUCTION

The construction of the three chip camera is not similar to that of the three tube camera. As explained in Chapter 10, in the three tube camera each one of the primary colors is created by an individual tube and associated channel processing circuits. Resolution is taken from the high frequency component of the green channel. One image chip per primary channel would not be effective for the three chip camera, because each image sensor has

a resolving power equal to one half of the photodiode spacing contained on its plane. This problem is known as signal aliasing. In a conventional tube camera, light is continuously falling on the target, and is continually being scanned by the beam. In chip cameras, the pickup element is separated by spacing. Therefore, there are areas on the surface where light is not detected. High resolution objects such as images that produce quick signal rise times cannot be clearly defined. Current technology limits the number of horizontal picture elements to approximately 384. The NEC SP-3A three chip camera uses a dual chip pickup system to produce the green signal. This dual chip system enables the camera to handle greater amounts of light and frequency bandwidth. The remaining chip can produce both red and blue color by means of a multiple stripe filter similar to that of the single tube color camera. The SP-3A dual green system attempts to imitate both the sensitivity and bandwidth of the human eye.

The optical system of the three chip camera contains a lens, dichroic (ND) filter and infrared (IR) cut filter similar to those of the three tube camera. In addition, the optics contain a glass low pass filter. This low pass filter is designed to suppress high frequencies that might cause aliasing. A dual chip green system is used, so the prisms must split the light into two green signals and one magenta signal. (The combination of red and green equals magenta.)

Because chips are much smaller and lighter than tubes, the imaging chips can be directly mounted to the optical assembly. Registration is permanently set at the factory, so adjustment is never required.

SIGNAL PROCESSING

In chip cameras, shift resistors driven by driver circuits replace the deflection circuits and deflection yokes used in the tube cameras. Clock rates for the SP-3A are 7.16 MHz or two times the subcarrier frequency. The green 1 and green 2 signals are clocked 180° out of

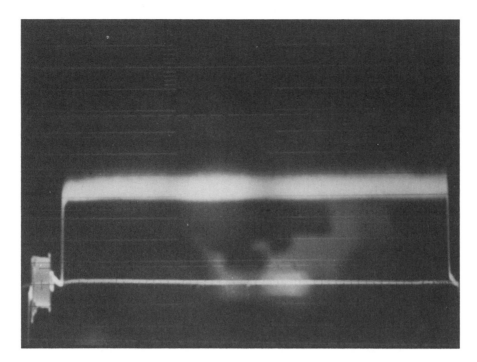

Tube Camera

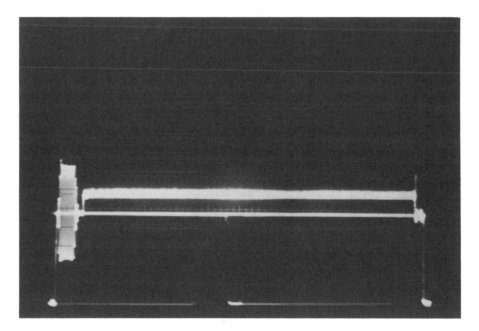

Chip Camera

Figure 11.3: Output signal of tube camera vs. output signal of chip camera.

phase and therefore can easily be separated. This is also true of the red and blue signals. Individual signal channel processing is achieved by a procedure of sample and hold. Greater chroma resolution is achieved by mixing the high frequency component of the green channel with the red and blue channels.

Chip cameras can preset gain balance with a one touch control that stores data in a non-volatile memory chip. In this way, information can be held forever, regardless of whether the power switch is on or off. Because the iris automatically closes during any power loss (a feature of most high quality cameras), black balance is performed each time the camera is turned on. After the black balance is completed, the iris reopens to the opening set by the auto iris circuit. These circuits eliminate the need for manual individual channel gain setup.

SINGLE ELEMENT CHIP CAMERAS

Hitachi uses a MOS chip as a pickup element for its single chip camera. A color mosaic is integrated into the chip itself. This system is similar to the color dichroic of the single tube color camera. The two primary filters are yellow and cyan; the third is green, which consists of a mixture of the yellow and cyan filter (yellow + cyan = green). The fourth filter is clear and yields a white signal (red + green + blue = white). The output of these four signals is amplified and matrixed into red and blue through the following process:

red = white − cyan = yellow − green
blue = white − yellow = cyan − green

The Y signal is generated by combining the four color filters.

Similar to the single tube color camera, high light levels can saturate the color filters of single element chip cameras, causing loss of stripe resolution and the picture to display the baseband green color. However, the four signal output line design of the single chip MOS device suppresses the saturation illumination by setting different video voltages for each output line. This causes the same saturation level to be achieved for each color.

CHIPS VS. TUBES

Current chip devices have many advantages over their tube counterparts. The major drawback of tubes is their inability to quickly accept and give up changes in scene images. The frame transfer characteristics of image chips alleviates this problem by clearing the image registers before they accept new information. No memory of the previous scene is held. For this reason, under low light conditions when lag in tubes increases, chip devices resolve greater detail, particularly when viewing moving objects. This also extends to shooting under low light conditions, during which the chip can see more detail and retain better color balance. In addition, the combination of frame transfer and blooming correction enables chip cameras to handle much greater light ranges than tube cameras. Chip camera resolution is expressed in terms of the number of picture elements present in each vertical and horizontal scan. A simplified method to determine a camera's horizontal resolution is to multiply the number of horizontal picture elements by .75. For example, 320 horizontal picture elements multiplied by .75 equals 240 horizontal lines of resolution. However, when dealing with the overall picture resolution, a combination of both vertical and horizontal picture elements exists. High resolution chips contain a greater number of vertical elements. Chip cameras have a spectral response that can extend out into the near infrared region. With the use of dichroic filtering, spectral response is maintained well within the visual range, and as the memory of the chip is cleared after each transfer cycle, lag is negligible. This also accounts for the chip's ability to clearly resolve fast moving objects without smearing.

Aside from beam transmission factors, electron movement across the CCD is not dependent on the use of deflection coils as it is in tube cameras. Electron movement across the face of the CCD is determined by the voltage applied to the electrodes. Because all the voltage is equal in potential, electrons move across the rows at the same time. As the potential at the beginning of the scan is the same at the end, no resolution loss or distortion occurs. (Figure 11.3 illustrates the difference in output signals of tube cameras versus chip cameras. Notice the evenness of transmission of the chip camera.)

From an operations standpoint, the CCD camera offers complete freedom from setup, and no registration adjustments are required because the chips are permanently mounted to the optical block assembly. Color stability is also less of a problem as the CCDs are more stable under varying environmental conditions.

Although the initial cost of a CCD camera will probably exceed that of a comparable tube camera, the situation is only temporary. Conventional cameras usually require tube changes within the first two years of operation, and the cost of repair can exceed the purchase price of a CCD camera. Users planning to maintain their cameras for more than four years might realize large savings by considering a CCD camera.

12 Camera Selection

Camera selection is usually a compromise between desired features and affordable price. With production requirements in mind, the following specifications and features should be reviewed before you decide on a camera.

CAMERA WEIGHT

Camera weight is an important consideration for both the ENG (electronic news gathering) and studio user. A camera should be light enough to be carried on your shoulder. For studio operation, heavy cameras require tripods, which add to system costs. Lack of weight, however, should not come at the expense of camera protection because there is always the possibility that a camera will be dropped. Die cast construction affords the best type of protection. Many camera manufacturers use aluminum structures to maintain minimal weight. (When considering camera weight and balance remember to include the weight of the camera's lens.)

POWER CONSUMPTION

Three Tube Cameras

Power consumption or battery operation determines how long the camera can maintain uninterrupted shooting. Consumption is usually rated in terms of watts (voltage × amperage). Many three tube cameras, due to their high power consumption, require a separate battery. ENG/EFP (electronic news gathering/electronic field production) shooting also requires the use of a videotape recorder. The battery operating time of the VCR should match that of the camera. Many camera manufacturers offer "quick charge" batteries, which cut down greatly on recharge time. When prolonged shooting is required, it is necessary to use two batteries alternately: one powering the camera, while the other is charged or used as a standby.

Single Tube Cameras

The normal operating point of a single tube camera is 12 volts. This low rate of power consumption (usually below 10 watts) allows the single tube camera to use a portable VCR's battery as a power source during remote shootings, removing the need for a separate battery. When determining the operating time of a single sourced camera and VCR unit, it is necessary to add together the power consumption of both items.

OPTICAL SYSTEM

Choosing between a prism and dichroic mirror optical system has become less of a user choice, since the cost of prism optics has dropped dramatically over the past few years. Mirror optics require one additional f-stop of light compared to prism optics. However, this disadvantage can be offset by the versatility of mirror optic cameras to accommodate a C mount lens. A C mount lens is generally less expensive than its bayonet counterpart. In addition, a C mount lens can be interchanged between single tube cameras.

COLOR CONVERSION AND WHITE BALANCE

Color conversion and white balance are a matter of control. The more controls, the better the white balance will be over a wide range of adverse lighting conditions. Three tube cameras have both optical and electronic methods of adjusting for white balance. If using an optical setting, the color conversion filter wheel should contain both a 5500° and 5500° + ND (neutral density) filter setting. The latter setting not only converts sunny light to 3200°, it also cuts down the amount of incoming light by 25%. This allows the camera to be used on extremely bright days without blooming.

BUILT-IN COLOR BARS

Internal color bar systems are important if you intend to use the color bars as the primary reference for setting up the videotape recorder.

Camera color bar systems may generate with full or split field color bars. Full field color bars have a white level of only 75 IRE. During VCR setup or repair, all adjustments are made to reference a 100 IRE level. Adjusting a recorder to a 75% IRE level can greatly affect its ability to perform to specifications.

Split field color bars, on the other hand, display both 75% IRE and 100% IRE levels, which allow cameras with split field color bar systems to serve as complete test fixtures in recording systems. With the use of split field color bars, the I & Q signals (see Chapter 9) are displayed, enabling more accurate camera encoder setup. Broadcast and high-end production systems use split field bars.

AUTOMATIC SETUP CIRCUITS

Automatic circuits offer operator ease during setup and speed when the camera needs to be reset under shooting conditions. Automatic control of registration and white balance reduces many complex adjustments to a single button. The camera's automatic circuits should include a battery backup system to maintain memory when the camera is powered down.

INTERNAL SYNC GENERATOR AND GENLOCK

Although sync is usually considered as a specification, blanking considerations have caused it to be viewed as a camera feature. All color cameras provide 2:1 interlaced sync. Specifications for sync are usually defined as follows:

• RS-170, which meets all the requirements to conform with minimum blanking standards.

• RS-170A, which in addition to having the same sync as RS-170, also contains provisions for adjustable horizontal and vertical blanking. This feature is a requirement for post-production work, because processing equipment distorts camera blanking.

• RS-170A with color framing. In addition to adjustable blanking, this type of sync generator maintains accurate horizontal to subcarrier phasing. This type of signal is best used by 1-inch recorders, which have a capacity for color framing input signals.

• Genlock. This is a method of synchronizing a camera's internal sync generator to an external video signal. Genlock is important when multiple cameras are used within a system configuration to avoid distortion when the cameras are switched.

ENCODER

The encoder specification will have more meaning to the broadcast engineer than it will to the video producer. Y, I and Q encoding systems offer more color bandwidth than R-y, B-y systems. However, when considering encoding, remember that all but the most expensive monitors decode color by means of a R-y, B-y system, which unfortunately negates the advantage of the Y, I and Q systems. More important than the signal quality of the Y, I and Q encoder is its ability to generate a split field color bar signal for camera and VCR setup.

GAIN BOOST

Gain boost is a feature used to boost the gain of the video signal when the camera is operating under low light conditions. Signal boost usually ranges between 6 to 12 db, or 9 to 18 db. Increasing the gain of the video signal +6 db doubles the gain of the signal. Increasing the gain of the video signal is not without

its drawbacks, however. All video signals contain noise. Additional noise is added to the video during signal processing. Boosting the gain is accomplished by adding stages of signal amplification. As a result, boosting the signal adds more noise to the video and reduces the camera's overall signal-to-noise ratio. The increased noise at the +12 db and +18 db levels can render the picture unusable. How much a video signal can be boosted and still be usable depends on the camera's initial signal-to-noise measurement. Signal-to-noise ratios of 56 db and higher can accommodate boosts of 18 db, while signal-to-noise ratios of between 52 db to 54 db are associated with an upper limit boost of +12 db. Low-end three tube cameras and single tube cameras with signal-to-noise specification of under 50 db usually have single stage db boosts of +6 db.

NEW FEATURES

Manufacturers are always improving on the features offered by their color cameras to either eliminate operating problems or extend the camera's operating range.

Hot Shoe Connections

External components, such as the lens, viewfinders, microphones and battery packs, are usually connected to the camera body via cable and connectors, which can break or interfere with user operations. Hot shoes eliminate the problems associated with cables and connectors by directly transferring signals from the camera body via its mounting connector.

Improved Dynamic Range

Since almost all cameras will be subject to adverse lighting conditions, camera manufacturers have increased the dynamic (contrast) range by providing processing circuits that compress increases of 300% in the video level

Figure 12.1: Sony DXC-3000 3-chip CCD color camera. Photo courtesy the Sony Corp.

Figure 12.2: NEC SP-3A3-chip CCD color camera. Photo courtesy the Broadcast Equipment Division, NEC America, Inc.

Figure 12.3: JVC KY-80U/KR-M260U 3-chip camera with camcorder. Photo courtesy JVC Company of America.

to the white peak level of 110%. In this way, details in the highlighted white areas can be seen.

CHOOSING THE CAMERA TO MEET YOUR NEEDS

The selection of a color camera is a matter of personal choice. Within any given price range, today's user has a wide selection of both single and three tube cameras. The type of camera you purchase is often determined by how you want to use it and how much you want to pay. When considering specifications, three tube plumbicon cameras offer the best picture quality under the widest range of lighting conditions. It is also the most expensive camera, both from the standpoint of initial purchase and tube replacement. Single tube cameras offer the advantages of low cost, compact construction and easy setup. (Figures 12.1, 12.2 and 12.3 illustrate some 3-chip CCD cameras available on the market today.)

Charts and test equipment are not required for camera evaluation. All color cameras look good under proper lighting conditions. This is usually the way cameras are demonstrated by dealers. You can perform your own evaluation by following the steps listed below.

1. Cap the camera lens. With the lens capped, beam current will be at its lowest level. The camera's video output will therefore be its dark current, which represents the signal and noise levels that can be expected in the camera's blacks. Under ideal conditions, the video output of a capped camera should be black and noise free. If the video looks gray and noisy, the camera most likely has a high dark current and low signal-to-noise specifications. In addition, if the overall video level is uneven, or if there are patches of dark and light, the quality of the camera's tube and yoke are probably not very good.

2. Focus the camera on a brown object. Under "sales" conditions, with the camera shooting at a pre-arranged scene, you will probably be hard pressed to find any brown objects. Practically all colors can be described in terms of saturation, brightness, lightness and brilliance, with the exception of brown. Brown is the result of a complicated perception of low luminance orange-yellow surfaces against an illuminated background. The human retina has a problem interpreting this color. As a result, brown is a hard color for both human perception and camera reproduction. Cameras that reproduce good browns should also have good individual color reproduction.

3. Operate the camera under low light conditions. Turn the camera on a low light level scene. Evaluate the amount of picture detail and noise. Next activate the gain boost. It will be a matter of personal judgment as to the acceptability of the picture under these conditions.

CONCLUSION

Once you have selected your camera, you will need to understand the operation of test equipment and camera setup procedures. These are discussed in the following chapters.

13 Test Equipment and Other Tools of the Trade

To properly operate or judge a camera's performance, it is important to understand test equipment. Hours, days or even months of production can be wasted if a color camera is setup improperly. In this chapter, we will review waveforms as they are read by waveform monitors and vectorscopes. To help the reader understand some of the discussions of equipment used in this chapter, we recommend a review of Chapter 1: The Foundation of the System.

THE WAVEFORM MONITOR

Reading the Faceplate

The NTSC television system is made up of 525 horizontal scanning lines divided into two fields of 262.5 horizontal lines each occurring at a vertical rate. The waveform monitor is used to measure the timing and amplitude of these vertical and horizontal lines. (See Figure 13.1.)

Video signals are expressed as volts, which are measured on the waveform monitor as IRE (Institute of Radio Engineers) units. The reference point for the IRE scale is the 0 IRE mark. The portion of the television signal that moves, in a positive direction from the 0 IRE point is the active video, or picture information. Signals moving in the negative direction from the 0 IRE point represent the blanking level to the lowest point of sync.

When related to signal voltages, 0 to 100 IRE units represent 0.714 volts. Within the range of active video, located between 0 and 20 IRE is the 7.5 IRE point, or pedestal level. It represents the blackest point of the active video signal. By setting the pedestal level no lower than 7.5 IRE, the darkest levels of a scene are protected from falling below the 0 IRE level. If this should occur, the monitor might mistake the video's pedestal for sync and begin a new horizontal field for active video. Because the 7.5 IRE level is the starting point of signal amplitude, it is referred to as the "setup level."

The negative transition from 0 to −40 IRE units equals 0.286 volts. Added to the 0.714 volts of the positive 0 to 100 IRE units, the total video signal can be referred to as a 1 volt peak-to-peak signal. (See Figure 13.2.)

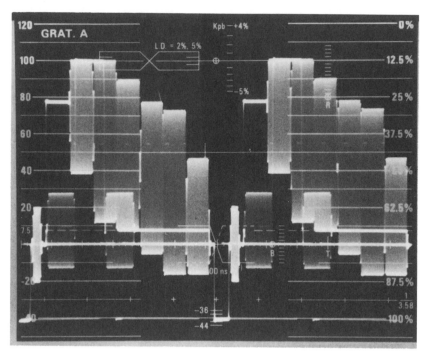

Figure 13.1: Two horizontal scan lines of NTSC split field color bars as viewed on a waveform monitor. Photo courtesy Tektronix, Inc.

Signal Level Limitations

Theoretically, the only limits on camera signal levels are those caused by the electronic construction of the camera itself. Most single tube, and all three tube color cameras provide controls for adjusting the amplitude and phase of sync signals. Prescripted limitations for sync and video levels maintain consistency between the camera and monitor. Sync levels are preset because the monitor references to a level of 0.286 volts. Limits on white level are due to carrier limits within the bandwidth of a television channel. In a closed circuit system, in which the signal is not transmitted by means of RF, the video levels over 100 IRE will cause loss of details in the high light areas. However, in RF transmission, as the video level increases, the RF carrier amplitude decreases. If the video level is not

limited, harmonies of the RF carrier can extend beyond 4.2 MHz. As the carrier approaches the 4.5 MHz sound carrier, there is a chance that the video can bleed into the audio and cause interference. Another way of looking at this situation is in terms of the carrier output. The amount of output carrier is determined by the strength of the modulating video signal. The higher the DC level of the video signal, the lower the carrier output. The value of the RF carrier at any given video level is represented by the right hand set of markings on the faceplate of the waveform monitor. (Refer to Figure 13.1.)

The lowest point of the sync signal is the maximum amount of carrier (100%) and therefore must be represented by the same value on every horizontal line. The blanking carrier represents 75% of the carrier. Reference white is considered to be, under normal conditions, the high-

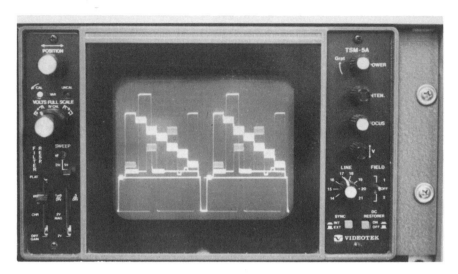

Figure 13.2: Waveform monitor displaying 1 volt peak-to-peak video signal.

est level of the video picture. Although the reference white level is not fixed on every horizontal line, it is important that it not exceed the 100 IRE level. This level represents 12.5% of the peak carrier value. Signals higher than this value will cause two undesirable effects. First, the carrier power drops so low that any type of noise can interfere with the quality of the receiver picture. Second, the lack of video carrier creates an insufficient 4.5 MHz audio carrier, which results in a buzzing sound as the video is "heard" in the audio.

The white level varies because of a number of factors (reflected light, lens opening, etc.). As the level changes, the camera system allows for transitions over the 100 IRE level. The camera's white level is usually set between 110 IRE to 120 IRE units. This is a 10% to 20% increase in signal level, which results in an additional 12.5% loss of carrier power that reduces it to zero. Continuing to operate at this level would render a picture unstable. It is therefore critical to monitor the camera's signal level with a waveform monitor during any video production.

Color Levels

Color signals have the addition of the back porch burst signals. The 0.3 volt burst signal is positioned between the −20 and +20 IRE levels. The television system sees the average of these burst sine waves as having an average level of 0 IRE, so there is no danger that the transition below 0 IRE will be mistaken for sync. Figure 13.3 illustrates the chroma and burst portions of the video signal as it is viewed on a waveform monitor.

Timing Measurements

The waveform monitor is also used to confirm signal pulse widths. To do this, the operating mode of the waveform monitor must be changed. During amplitude measurement, the waveform monitor's sweep is set to display two horizontal lines (2H). To measure signal timing, the sweep is changed to show one microsecond per division (1 us/div.) In this setting, the larger divisions located at the IRE line represent one mic-

Table 13.1: Primary Waveform Timing Measurements for Horizontal Blanking

Horizontal Blanking: 10.5 microsecond to 11.4 microsecond, measured from the leading edge of one active line of video to the trailing edge of the next horizontal line of active video. Measurements are taken from the active video to the + 4 IRE level.

Horizontal Sync Width: 4.45 microsecond to 5.08 microsecond, measured from the leading edge of the front porch to the trailing edge of the back porch.

Breezeway: Not less than 0.381 microseconds, measured from the − 4 IRE level to the first point, where the first cycle of burst crosses the 0 IRE point.

Burst: The burst signal is measured in terms of cycles instead of actual duration. Burst requires a minimum of 8 cycles. The first cycle of burst is defined at the point where the first half cycle exceeds 50% of the peak amplitude. The end of burst is defined as the last cycle whose amplitude exceeds 50% of the peak amplitude. (Remember that all amplitude measurements are taken from the 0 IRE point.)

Table 13.2: Primary Waveform Timing Measurements for Vertical Blanking

Vertical Blanking: Nineteen to 21 horizontal lines. This measurement is taken from the leading edge of the first equalization pulse to the trailing edge of the last equalization pulse. These pulses can be easily recognized as having a duration that is double that of the regular horizontal pulses. They are used to maintain horizontal sync during the long transition of vertical blanking. The timing equivalent of the 19 to 21 horizontal line duration is approximately 1.17 milliseconds to 1.33 milliseconds. As with horizontal blanking, the measurement is taken from the + 4 IRE level.

Vertical Sync: Three horizontal lines. As the vertical sync is contained within the vertical blanking, each horizontal line is composed of two equalization pulses, so the duration of vertical sync may be counted as six equalization pulses. The width of vertical sync is equal to 1.5 milliseconds.

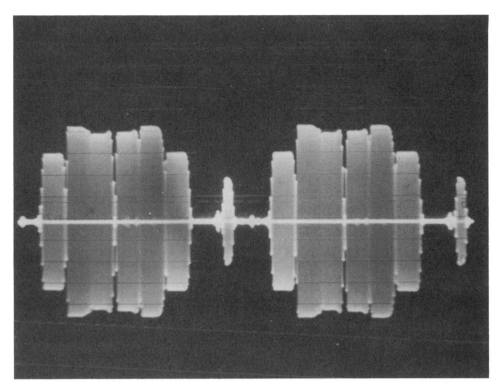

Figure 13.3: Chroma and burst positions of the video signal as viewed on a waveform monitor.

rosecond, while the shorter division markings represent of 0.2 microseconds. The primary timing measurements are listed in Table 13.1.

To measure vertical blanking, adjust the monitor's sweep control to a magnified two line vertical sweep (2 V Mag.). See Figure 13.4. The primary timing measurements for vertical blanking are listed in Table 13.2.

The Response Mode

After timing measurements have been taken, you may wish to use the two vertical sweep modes of the waveform monitor. This mode allows you to observe one complete frame of video. (See Figure 13.5). Although timing dura-

tions are hard to see, it can be used to show problems that occur over long periods of time. The second waveform monitor mode is known as the RESPONSE MODE. (All timing and amplitude measurements can be made in the FLAT MODE which displays all aspects of the signal.) In some cases, when attempting to take amplitude measurements of a color signal, the chroma (which, like a burst signal, is a 3.58 MHz sine wave) can distort the reading. For this reason, the operator may choose to use the IRE response position to filter the burst and chroma information. If the operator needs to view only the 3.58 MHz information, the chroma response mode can be used.

The final operational mode on the waveform monitor is the differential gain (Diff Gain). This

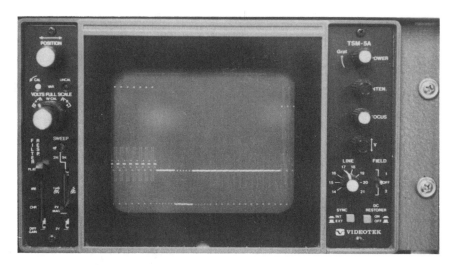

Figure 13.4: Magnified two line vertical sweep (2V mag.) as viewed on a waveform monitor.

measurement shows the relationship between chroma and luminance amplitude. For normal operations, there should be no change in chroma amplitude, as its DC value increases. Because this is a function of the camera's encoder, the measurement is usually taken from the camera's internal color bar generator.

THE OSCILLOSCOPE

The oscilloscope (See Figure 13.6) can perform most of the functions of the waveform monitor, as well as probe individual areas throughout the camera system. Whether you choose to use an oscilloscope instead of a waveform monitor is a matter of personal preference.

Waveform monitors lock on at the signal input and have a faceplate that allows the operator to determine signal pulse and width. Oscillocopes need to be triggered on the input signal or referenced to an external signal by means of a separate input. The faceplate readings, rather than being fixed, can be varied by means of amplitude and width settings. Readings at the horizontal rate are taken by the microsecond settings. Vertical rates are taken by the millisecond settings.

The greatest asset of the oscilloscope is its ability to display more than one signal at a time. Almost all of today's scopes have dual trace capability, and many permit third channel trigger view. Use of these features gives the operator the ability to view changes in signals from one point to another, or to compare signals that work in conjunction with each other.

Details of oscilloscope operations extend beyond the scope of this book. In Chapter 14, we will describe the settings used for camera adjustments. In general, however, if you do plan to use an oscilloscope in place of a waveform monitor, remember that the input signal to the scope must be terminated in 75 ohms. This can be done by using a tee connector and terminating one end in 75 ohms, or continuing the cable run to a device that terminates in 75 ohms, such as a monitor.

Table 13.3 lists settings for the oscilloscope.

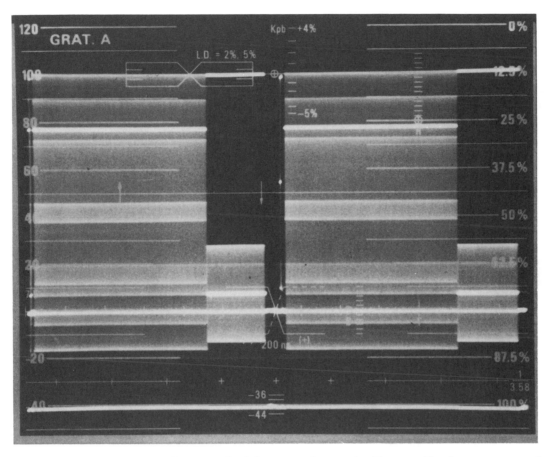

Figure 13.5: One complete frame of video as shown in the vertical sweep mode of a waveform monitor. Photo courtesy Tektronix, Inc.

THE VECTORSCOPE

Although the waveform monitor will indicate the presence of a color signal by showing whether or not it contains burst, it is unable to indicate the phase of the signal. It is the relationship of the chroma to the burst that determines the hue of the television picture. The first function of the vectorscope is to show chroma and burst phase. While a waveform monitor indicates luminance in terms of voltage levels, the vectorscope shows the strength of the color signal in terms of saturation.

In Chapter 8, we discussed the theory of color, which is relevant to the operation of the vectorscope. If we pick a primary color starting point, such as green, we can trace the additive and subtractive primary and secondary relationships around the color circle until we return to green. Different primary and secondary colors can be expressed as different points on this circle. Studies have shown that if we pick any point on

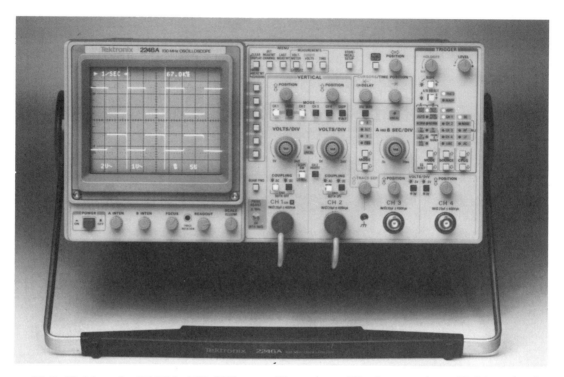

Figure 13.6: Tektronix 2246A 100-MHz oscilloscope. Photo courtesy Tektronix, Inc.

the circle as a reference color, the human eye will perceive a color change if we move approximately 3.6° in any direction from that point. Because of the additive process of primary colors, each secondary color is the result of two primary colors that have been added together. For example:

Green + Blue = Cyan, which is positioned between green and blue on the color circle.
Blue + Red = Magenta, which is positioned between blue and red on the color circle.

Red + Green = Yellow, which is positioned between red and green on the color circle.

On the vectorscope, burst is used as the color reference point, and is located at the 180° point. The correct phase and saturation for each color is noted on the vectorscope faceplate by a group of boxes located to the left of the faceplate in Figure 13.7. For color phasing, the inner boxes represent a phase difference of + 1 − 2.5°. The outer boxes show a phase difference of +/− 10°. (Note that the 2.5° represented by the vec-

Table 13.3: Oscilloscope Settings

Channel one	Input video terminated in 75 ohms.
Trigger	Horizontal sync or self trigger on channel one.
Volts per division	1 volt per division.
Time per division	0 or 20 microseconds per division.

Viewing Vertical Waveforms:

Trigger	Vertical sync or self trigger to video on channel one.
Volts per division	1 volt per division.
Time per division	5 milliseconds per division.

Delay Mode Operation:

Trigger	Set according to the rate of signal you wish to view—horizontal or vertical.
Time base selection	Use the main time base to view the complete waveform and delayed sweep to view the internal part of the waveform.
Select	A and B alternate sweep function. Turn down the scope intensity. The delayed section of the sweep will be highlighted. Use the delay time mode to move the sweep to the desired part of the sweep. Press the delay mode to completely view the delay signal.

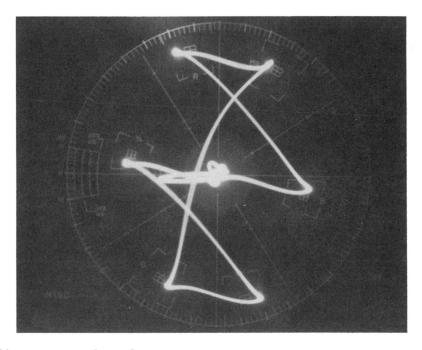

Figure 13.7: Vectorscope faceplate.

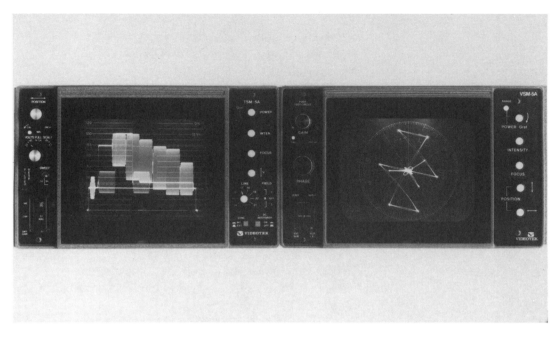

Figure 13.8: Videotek model TSM-5A waveform monitor and model VSM-5A vectorscope used in tandem. Photo courtesy of Videotek, Inc.

torscope's setup are within the 3.5° phase limits of hue shifts sensed by the human eye.)

For saturation adjustments, the inner boxes on the vectorscope screen represent changes of 2.5 IRE units and the outer boxes represent changes of 20 IRE units. Using the waveform monitor, we were able to check differences in chroma due to changes in luminance levels. With the vectorscope, we can check changes in chroma phase, which are caused by changes in saturation. A series of additional boxes used to indicate shifts of 10° above and below the 180°/0° points. Shifts to the plus and minus sides can

also be used to determine differential phase.

CONCLUSION

Figure 13.8 illustrates how the waveform monitor and vectorscope can be used in tandem to measure the video signal. Knowing how to operate the waveform monitor, vectorscope and oscilloscope is just the beginning of understanding their various uses. In Chapter 14 we will use these tools of the trade to perform the technical step-by-step procedure for setting up a color camera.

14 Setting Up The Camera

In this chapter we will discuss procedures for setting up three tube and single tube cameras, as well as the adjustment and alignment specifications to be used with test equipment.

We again remind you that this material should be considered as a general guide. Circuit descriptions and alignment procedures for specific cameras can be found in the manufacturer's manual.

It is recommended that all alignment procedures be performed under 3200° Kelvin lights, set to the level required by the camera's sensitivity specification. Remember to check the setting of the camera's color wheel. During camera setup, the color filter must pass the 3200° Kelvin light without altering the color content of the light. For this reason, the 3200° filter setting is usually clear glass, or nothing at all.

To achieve uniform lighting conditions, it is recommended that you use two lamps angled toward the test object. To determine lighting uniformity, use a light meter to measure the light around the perimeter of the test object. (See Figure 14.1.)

TEST CHARTS

Test objects are usually test charts. Depending on the subject matter, test charts can be used for camera setup as well as for determining camera specifications and detailed alignments. For three tube camera setup, the most commonly used charts are the registration (see Figures 14.2 and 14.3) and black-and-white log reflectance charts. The registration chart is used to align the red, green and blue tubes. The reflectance chart is used to adjust color balance so black-and-white objects will appear as such to the color camera.

GENERAL SETUP

Camera setup begins with the test equipment. The video output of the camera should be routed to the waveform monitor, vectorscope and color output monitor. If your camera has test monitor capability, connect this output to a black-and-white monitor. This test output is used for registration adjustments.

The last piece of test equipment in the video

chain must be terminated in 75 ohms. All test equipment that the video signal "loops through" must be "unterminated." Failure to properly terminate video lines will cause the camera's output to appear greatly distorted. Unterminated lines expand the video and sync levels, causing the picture to appear excessively bright. Double terminated lines suppress the video and sync levels causing the picture to appear dark. After the video line has been properly terminated, the test equipment can be calibrated.

CALIBRATING TEST EQUIPMENT

Waveform Monitor Setup

The following steps should be followed for proper waveform monitor setup (see Figure 14.4):
1. Allow the waveform monitor to warm up for at least 15 minutes.
2. Rotate the intensity control clockwise until the trace is set at the desired brightness. Be careful not to turn the intensity control up to its full brightness position. Operating the waveform monitor's CRT for long periods of time at full brightness can greatly reduce its life.
3. Use the vertical position control on the trace to place the beam on the 0 IRE graticule line. Use the horizontal position to start the beam trace at the first major division mark on the 0 IRE graticule line—located on the operator's left side of the waveform.
4. Set the VOLTS FULL SCALE switch to the 1V CAL position. Use the vertical position control to vertically center the display in the − 40 IRE to 100 IRE unit area of the graticule. This calibrator waveform sets the lower (sync tip) and upper (white peak) limits on the video signal.
5. If the calibrator signal appears to lack definition, adjust the astigmatism and focus controls to obtain a well defined waveform.

(Note: The oscilloscope can perform most of the functions of the waveform monitor. Whether you choose to use an oscilloscope instead of a waveform monitor is a matter of personal preference.)

Vectorscope Setup

Use the following procedure to set up the vectorscope (See Figure 14.5.):
1. With no signal input, adjust the intensity until the beam can be seen. Be careful not to turn up the intensity level too high on the CRT. Allow the vectorscope at least 15 minutes to warm up.
2. Use the focus control to obtain the best defined beam.
3. Use the horizontal and vertical position controls to move the beam to the crosspoint of the horizontal and vertical graticules.
4. Depress the mode select button (gain control) twice. The test circle will appear. Confirm that the circles are concentric with each other and that the outer most circle is equal with the graticule circle.
5. Set the camera's output signal to color bars. This is where the camera becomes a test generator. Use the signal to confirm that the individual colors fall within their appropriate 2.5° and 2.5 IRE graticule boxes. The burst signal should be found directly on the 0, 180° line. If the total color bar signal appears to be shifted in position, use the vectorscope's phase control, using the burst signal as a reference.

Monitor Setup

Prior to setting up the color video monitor, recheck the signals on the waveform monitor and vectorscope to confirm that the signal levels are properly set. If any deviation is found in the sync level of the waveform monitor and/ or burst level of the vectorscope, recheck your cable termination before proceeding.

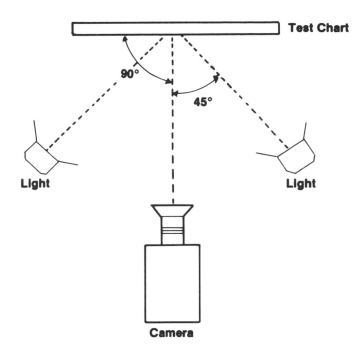

Figure 14.1: Typical arrangement of camera, test chart and lights.

Many monitors are used as test fixtures as well for viewing. When relying on the monitor to judge a camera's color reproduction, it is important that the color balance of the monitor be correct. This adjustment can be performed only if your monitor has adjustments for the three individual red, blue and green guns.

Begin this procedure by adjusting the monitor's brightness, chroma and phase controls. Input the camera's color bar signal and set up the monitor's controls using the following procedure.

1. Turn off all monitor presets and turn down the chroma control to its lowest position.
2. Adjust the brightness control until all levels of the individual color bars can clearly be seen.
3. Adjust the chroma level until color can be seen.
4. Adjust the phase control until the yellow bar appears to have the purest hue, or

most yellow appearance. (Yellow is selected because shooting usually centers around people. A good yellow adjustment provides the best skin tones.)

White Balance

The perception of white differs for each individual under different viewing conditions. Depending on the conditions, white can appear greenish, reddish, yellowish, etc. It is therefore necessary to define a value for absolute white. The standard for NTSC monitors is approximately 9300° Kelvin.

To adjust a monitor's white balance do the following:

1. Set the color monitor to monochrome.
2. Place the monitor in the SETUP or TEST mode. This switch suppresses the horizontal scan to a single line.
3. Turn off the red and blue channel guns. Adjust the gain of the green channel

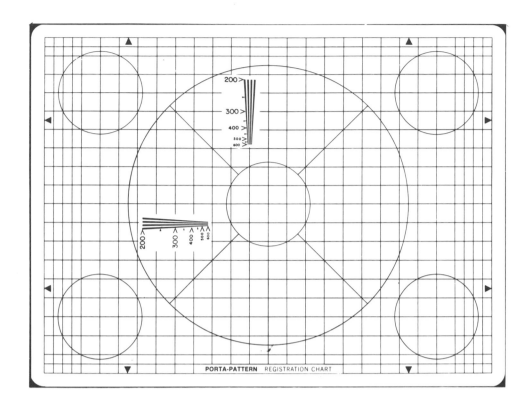

Figure 14.2: Registration Chart. Courtesy Porta-Pattern, Inc.

Figure 14.3: Log Reflectance Chart. Courtesy Porta-Pattern, Inc.

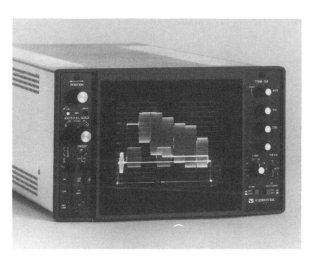

Figure 14.4: Model TSM-5A waveform monitor. Courtesy, Videotek, Inc.

Figure 14.5: Model 1720 Vectorscope. Courtesy Tektronix, Inc.

until you can see a complete line. Turn off the green gun and repeat this adjustment using the blue and red channel gains. If all gains are set to be uniform, the combination of red, blue and green will produce a white line. If the line has the tint of a particular color, lower its gain.

Convergence

In addition to making color balance adjustments, with high grade monitors you can also align the scan of the camera's individual guns. Called convergence, this adjustment is similar to camera registration. While viewing the color bar signals with the monitor set to the mono mode, check to see that the transition point between the bars are clearly defined by a single line. This check is limited to horizontal resolution errors. Some monitors contain an internal test signal generator bar that automatically adjusts convergence, making these manual adjustments unnecessary. However, it is a good idea to check the monitor's convergence so that monitor scanning errors will not frustrate you during camera setup and registration.

When monitor setup is complete, put the monitor in the color mode, and switch the camera from the color bar to the operation mode.

CAMERA CIRCUIT DESCRIPTION

Before we begin the actual alignment procedures for color cameras, the following review of the functions of camera circuitry should prove helpful.

Most three tube color and industrial single tube color cameras are used for both studio and ENG (electronic news gathering) work. So they can be used for both applications, the cameras' main power supplies are external to the camera. Camera head input voltage requirements are, therefore, limited to +12 volts D.C. This voltage is regulated down to the operating voltages required by the individual camera circuits. Typical voltages are −9 volts, +9 volts and +9.5 volts.

When the sync generator receives the proper voltage, it begins to generate sync signals. The output sync signal from the generator, usually a single integrated circuit, is used for the functions described below.

Horizontal Sync

The horizontal sync signal performs the following functions:
- Horizontali deflection, used in the shading and deflection circuits.
- Horizontal drive, used to drive the high voltage power supply.
- Vertical drive, used in the vertical deflection circuits.
- Composite sync, a combination of horizontal and vertical sync, used in the encoder circuits, and to provide sync to the final output stage of video.
- Burst, a 3.58 MHz signal used in the encoder circuit to create the system's color reference.

High Voltage Power Supply

The horizontal drive from the sync generator is inputted to a flip-flop circuit that provides an "alternating" voltage to the primary window of a transformer whose secondary window provides the various high voltages needed by the pickup tubes, focus and deflection circuits. It also provides the negative voltage to the tube's cathode.

Deflection Circuits

Vertical and horizontal sync are coupled to the deflection coils of the tube's yoke assemblies. Each adjustment responsible for camera registration is located on this board. In addition to providing signals to the deflection circuits, the horizontal and vertical drives are waveshaped into sawtooth and parabolic waveforms by a series of integrators, which are coupled into the tube's static shading correction circuits.

Video Processing Circuits

Video processing begins when the signal from the target contact is amplified through an FET and preamplifier. Besides providing amplification, the preamplifier is responsible for the system's frequency response, resolution and signal-to-noise ratio.

From the preamplifier stage, the signal enters the processor on a board where dynamic or target shading corrects defects due to the uneven light response of the camera's optical system. Horizontal sync is used to provide a D.C. reference for each of the channel signals, while a clamp pulse derived from the horizontal sync is used to create the tube's pedestal level.

The task of video processing is usually divided between two circuits. The first video processing board handles dynamic shading, D.C. clamping and the white level chip. The second processing circuit is usually responsible for signal gamma corrections and contouring. Gamma compensation is required to counterbalance the distortions of input voltage to output luminance created by the CRT. Each of the camera's color channels must be adjusted to have the same gamma curve. The midpoint or "knee" of the video signal is usually used as the reference for gamma setup.

Contouring signals contain a combination of vertical and horizontal signal components. They are required because the relationship between the beam diameter and the individual photoelectric cells of the target cause a loss of signal detail. Contouring is sometimes referred to as "aperture" or "detail." It is accomplished by delaying the video signal in the horizontal or vertical rate, and then remixing the signal with a one horizontal line delay. The delayed and non-delayed signals are mixed, adding the high frequency components of each, thereby increasing overall picture detail.

The R, G and B signals are coupled into the encoder circuit. This circuit mixes the channel outputs with sync, amplifies the Y (luminance) signal, and mixes it with chroma, either as Y, I and Q, or a R-y, B-y encoded signal.

Auto Control Circuits

Automatic circuitry can be limited to maintaining white levels, black levels, white and black levels and registration. In general, the automatic circuits operate by remembering preset voltages, which are then used to control the individual video or registration controls. The circuit self-checks each channel for its unity setting.

ALIGNING THE THREE TUBE COLOR CAMERA

Camera electronics can be broken down into two separate systems: one for deflection, the other for signal processing. During camera alignment both circuits are adjusted. Deflec-

tion circuit adjustments have priority, however, because they provide a signal to the processing circuits.

Check the camera power supply before making any adjustments. Proper camera performance depends on each circuit operating at its prescribed voltage. Power supply problems or misadjustments can lead to problems in obtaining correct signals. This is particularly true of the deflection circuits.

How well sync and encoder settings are maintained depends on the stability of the camera components. Misadjustment or defects in these circuits can seriously affect camera operations. The vertical and horizontal signals generated by the sync circuit are used by the deflection circuits to control beam scanning. The encoder circuit will determine the brightness, saturation, hue and purity of the output video. For these reasons, the sync and encoding circuits must be checked prior to deflection and tube channel gain adjustments. Table 14.1 lists adjustments for three tube camera setup, beginning with sync level and width checks.

Tube Registration

Once the operational setup of the camera is complete, the tubes should be registered. To register the blue and red tubes, we will assume that the green tube has not been changed, and therefore can be used as a reference.

During the operational registration setup, we adjusted the red and blue tube centering controls to match that of the green channel. These adjustments are effective only if each channel has the same horizontal and vertical size, linearity, rotation and skew. The goal of registration is to have each tube scan the same place at the same time.

Light has a great affect in the perception of registration errors. Incoming light can mask registration problems in high light areas. Because of this, the iris setting should be changed to reduce the incoming light by approximately 30%

(Continues on page 151.)

Table 14.1: Three Tube Camera Adjustments

SYNC LEVEL AND WIDTH CHECKS

Test Point:	Camera video output
Test Condition:	Camera set to color bars. (The camera's internal color bar generator is very useful here.)
Test Equipment:	Waveform monitor.
Equipment Setting:	Response to IRE. The IRE waveform monitor setting will filter out the 3.58 MHz subcarrier that might distort our ability to determine actual levels.
Sweep:	2H or 1H (if your waveform monitor has a 1H setting).

Adjustment	Setting or Check
Y Level (luminance level)	100 IRE or 0.714 volts peak to peak
Sync Level	40 IRE or 0.286 volts peak to peak
Setup Level (black level or pedestal level)	7.5 IRE or 0.53 volts peak to peak
Horizontal Blanking Width	Change waveform monitor setting: Sweep: 1 microsecond/division
H Blanking	Minimum setting to 10.8 microsecond
Breezeway	Change waveform monitor setting: Response: Flat to view the 3.58 MHz subcarrier.
Breezeway (burst start)	Separation of 0.381 microsecond from the rise of H sync to the start of the first cycle of burst.
Vertical Blanking Width	Change waveform monitor setting: Sweep: 2V Mag. (magnified)
V Blanking	Set to a minimum of 19 H lines (remember to count two equalization pulses as one horizontal line).

ENCODER ADJUSTMENTS

Test Point:	Camera video output
Test Condition:	Camera set to color bars
Test Equipment:	Waveform monitor
Equipment Settings:	Response: Flat
	Sweep: 1 microsecond/division

Adjustment	Setting or Check
Burst Level	Set to fall between + 20 IRE and − 20 IRE units. (0.3 volts peak to peak)

(Alternate Method):

Test Equipment:	Vectorscope
Equipment Setting:	Phase reference A
	Input A (For this example, we will assume the video is Input A)

Table 14.1: Three Tube Camera Adjustments (Cont.)

Adjustment	Setting or Check
Burst Phase	Set the Phase Control of the vectorscope so it aligns the burst with the 180°, zero line.
Burst Level	Set for 75% marking.
Test Equipment:	Waveform monitor
Equipment Setup:	Response: Flat
	Sweep: 2H or 1H

- -

Adjustment	Setting or Check
I & Q Carrier Balance	Locate the white and black (pedestal) signals. Turn the carrier balances alternately so the amount of subcarrier (3.58 MHz) signal is reduced.

(Alternate Method):

Test Equipment:	Vectorscope
Equipment Setting:	Gain to maximum
I & Q Carrier Balance	View the centerpoint of the display. Turn the controls so the spot moves to the crosspoint of the axis (chrominance becomes minimum).
Equipment Setting:	Gain to calibration
	Phase: Check to see that Burst is resting on the 180°, zero line.

Adjustment	Setting or Check
Chroma Gain	Set the chroma gain so the color vectors fall into their respective boxes on the vectorscope.

(Alternate Method for I and Q Encoded Cameras):

Adjustment	Setting or Check
I Axis Gain	Switch off the Q signal. Adjust the I axis so that the six spots of the axis position directly on the six I axis points of the vectorscope. (The I axis aligns with the highest resolution of the chroma signal. For this reason, always adjust the gain of the I axis first and then the Q axis).

Q AXIS GAIN ADJUSTMENT

Test Equipment:	Vectorscope
Setting:	Reference to Q axis
Gain:	Calibrate position.
	Adjust the Q gain so that the six Q axis spots align exactly with the six spots of the vectorscope Q axis.

QUADRATURE ADJUSTMENT (PHASE ADJUSTMENT) FOR I & Q ENCODED CAMERAS ONLY

I Axis Adjustment	I axis is on.
	Q axis is off.

Table 14.1: Three Tube Camera Adjustments (Cont.)

Adjustments	Setting or Check
I Axis Quadrature	Adjust, so it is superimposed on the I axis of the vectorscope.
Q Axis Adjustment	Confirm that the I axis and Q axis are perpendicular to each other.

DEFLECTION ADJUSTMENT

| Target: | Set up the target voltage of each of the tubes according to the manufacturer's tube rating. This adjustment can either be done with a DVM (digital volt meter) or with an oscilloscope set to read D.C. This adjustment is sometimes known as the cathode blanking pulse adjustment because the positive target potential is being set to overcome the negative cathode blanking pulse. |
| Adjustment Point: | The output leg of the target control. |

FOCUS ADJUSTMENT

Camera Lens Setting:	Iris to its widest opening, the smallest f-stop number.
Test Chart:	Registration, resolution or depth of modulation. (Refer to Figure 14.2 and see Figures 14.6 & 14.7)
Test Point:	Observe the signal from the monitor or test output.
Procedure:	Select the G output with the test encoder switch. Zoom the lens in to its maximum close-up position, and adjust to the best focus. Zoom out and adjust the lens back focus (flangeback) to obtain the best focus. After the lens focus is setup, try not to make any changes because it serves as the reference for individual tube focus.

TUBE FOCUS

Camera Lens:	Set the lens to the sensitivity specification (usually f-5.6)
Test Point:	Observe the signal from the monitor or test output.
Procedure:	1. Loosen the G locking screw (G lock).
	2. Adjust the back focus of the green channel by turning the "back focus" adjustment screw.
	3. Zoom the lens in and out to confirm that focus is maintained (lens tracking).
	4. Zoom the lens in and adjust the electronic focus to obtain the best focus. (If a depth of modulation chart is used, frame the chart and observe the video output on a waveform monitor. Adjust the focus to maximize the amplitude of each of the bursts. (See Figure 14.8)

Red and Blue Tube Back Focus

| Red Tube: | Change the test monitor signal output to red and repeat the procedure for tube mechanical and electronic focus. |
| Blue Tube: | Change the test monitor output to blue and repeat the setup procedure. |

TARGET CURRENT

Camera Lens:	Set the lens to the widest opening.
Test Chart:	Logarithmic gray scale. (See Figures 14.9 and 14.10.)
Test Point:	Output of the first stage video processor amplifier.

Table 14.1: Three Tube Camera Adjustments (Cont.)

Test Equipment:	Oscilloscope set to observe H rate (10 or 20 microsecond)
Procedure:	Turn the beam control until the white chip unfolds. Move the scope probe from under the green to the red and blue first stage amplifier outputs. Repeat the adjustment using the red and blue beam controls. (During this procedure, the amount of beam current that will be accepted by target is set up. It is also important to take into account that the camera must be able to resolve images in high light situations.)

BEAM ALIGNMENT

Camera Lens:	Set to the sensitivity specification (f-5.6)
Test Chart:	Registration chart.
Test Point:	Output of test or monitor output.
Test Setting:	Start with the switch set to the G position.
Procedure:	The purpose of the deflection magnets and coils is to center the beam on the target. The angle of impact must be 90°. To confirm that the deflection circuits are set correctly, vary the tube channel focus. As the beam moves away from the center of the tube, the 90° beam center relationship with the target should not change. Tube focus can be read by feeding an oscillator signal into the focus circuit, or by using the camera's internal oscillator—called focus warble. You can also vary the focus current by varying the focus control. When this method is used, make sure that the focus control returns to its previous setting after the adjustment is completed. If the center of the picture moves, adjust the V and H alignment controls until the center is stable.

Red and Blue Tube

Beam Alignment:	Repeat the procedure for beam, switching the monitor test output to the red output for red adjustment and to blue for blue adjustment.

during registration adjustments. The procedure for tube registration is outlined in Table 14.2.

After all the vertical lines of the red and blue tubes have been superimposed at the center of the outer edges, as described in Table 14.2, the individual tubes may appear to be out of adjustment. These differences are known as size and linearity. Horizontal size, in some cases also known as horizontal amplitude, will vary the distance of each of the registration chart's vertical lines. Vertical size, sometimes called vertical amplitude, will vary the distance of each of the registration chart's horizontal lines. While these adjustments may vary the overall size of the tube scan, linearity adjustments vary the proportion of the edges of the tube as compared with the tube's center scan width.

Other Deflection Adjustments

Other types of deflection adjustments are contained on more expensive color cameras. Some of these are listed below:

V-Bow	H-Bow
V-Trapezoidal	H-Trapezoidal
V-Pincushion	H-Pincushion

Green Tube Registration

Adjustments made to the red and blue tubes were done using the green channel as a reference. The question now arises, what happens when we change the green tube? When this occurs, we lose our registration reference. To

(Continues on page 157.)

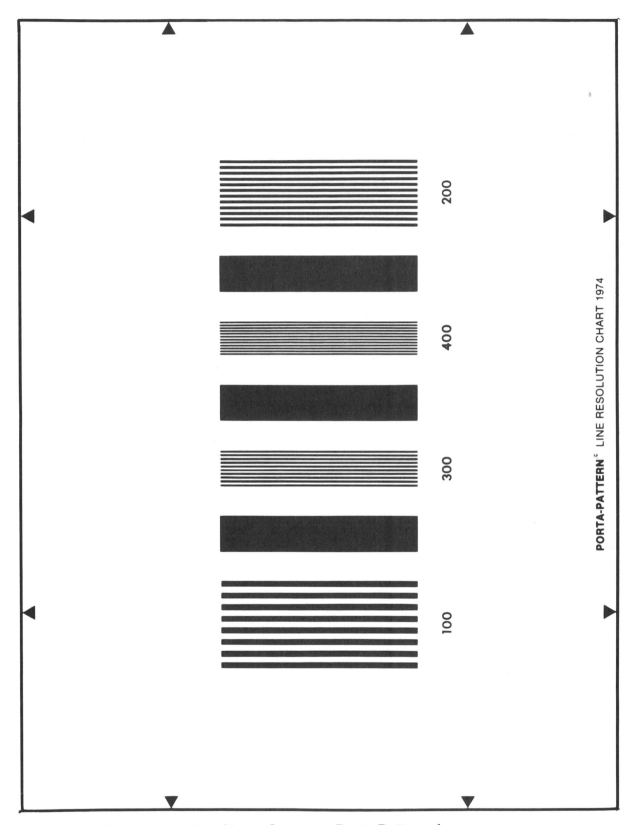

Figure 14.6: Line Resolution Chart. Courtesy Porta-Pattern, Inc.

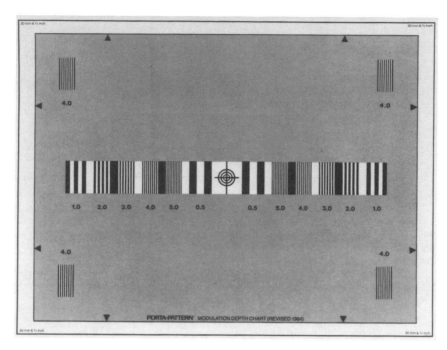

Figure 14.7: Modulation Depth Chart. Courtesy Porta-Pattern, Inc.

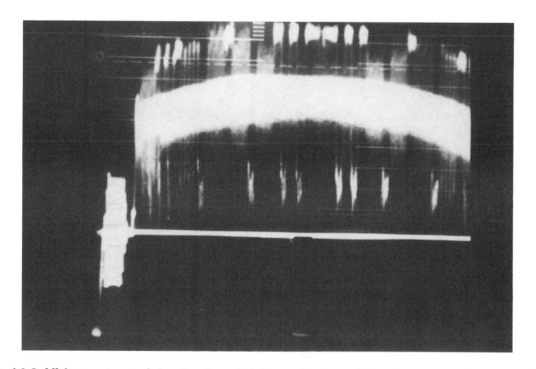

Figure 14.8: Video output of depth of modulation chart as viewed on a waveform monitor.

Figure 14.9: Eleven-stop Logarithmic Grey Scale Chart. Courtesy Porta-Pattern, Inc.

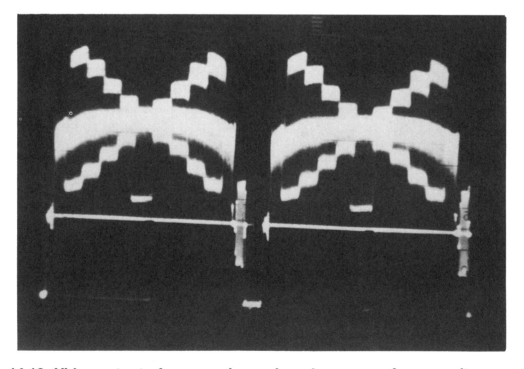

Figure 14.10: Video output of grey scale as viewed on a waveform monitor.

Table 14.2: Tube Registration Adjustment

Lens Setting:	f-4 or f-5.6, whichever brings the video output level below the 100 IRE mark.
Test Equipment:	Black-and-white monitor.
Test Output:	Test or monitor output of color camera.
Switch Settings:	G/ − G: Set to the − G position. Channel output: Set to either blue or red, depending on which tube you want to register first.

Yoke Rotation: Loosen the yoke locking screw and turn the rotation screw until the tube is on the same plane as the green tube.
After this adjustment has been completed, retighten the yoke lock screw. Because this lock screw is also responsible for maintaining tube back focus, it is recommended that you recheck the back focus after this adjustment is completed. (See Figures 14.11 and 14.12.)

Centering Adjustment:

Controls: Blue H centering (shift)
Red H centering (shift)
Blue V centering (shift)
Red V centering (shift)
(Some cameras repeat the centering adjustment on their deflection board. This helps to broaden the range of operator controls. If this is the case with your camera, set the operator controls to their center position prior to doing this adjustment. Use the deflection board controls to superimpose the two images at their centers.)

Skew Adjustments:

Controls: B-skew
R-skew
If the vertical lines cross only at the center and appear on opposite sides of the top and bottom of the vertical green center line, then a skew adjustment is required. After electronically rotating the red and blue skew, it is possible that the center lines may appear to be separated. If this is the case, repeat the centering adjustment.

Horizontal and Vertical Size and Linearity Adjustments:

Controls: H-size:
H-linearity (some cameras have linearity-1 and linearity-2 adjustments)
V-size:
V-linearity (some cameras have linearity-1 and linearity-2 adjustments.)

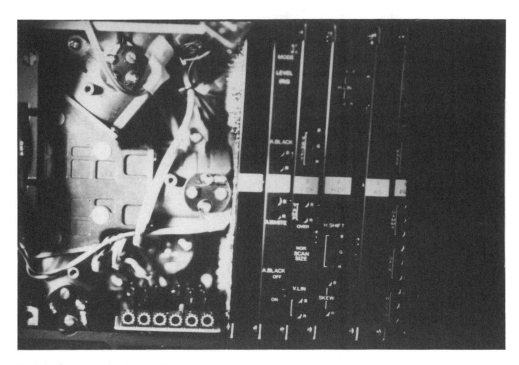

Figure 14.11: Internal view of three tube camera.

Figure 14.12: Close-up of yoke locking and rotation screws used for back focus adjustment.

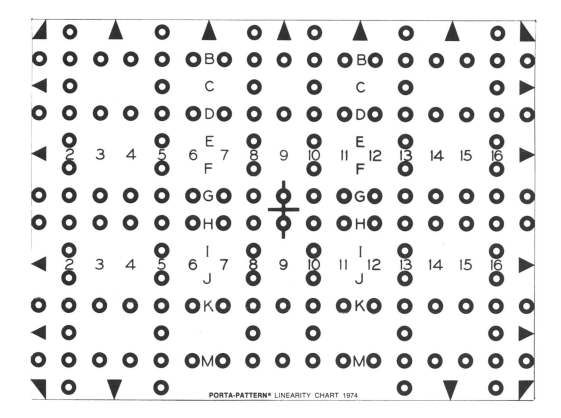

Figure 14.13: Linearity Chart. Courtesy Porta-Pattern, Inc.

align the green tube, we must focus on an object of known proportion and reference it to a scale of known proportions. The linearity chart, sometimes called the "ball" chart, is used as the reference object (see Figure 14.13). An external crosshatch generator is used to provide the reference signal. The procedure is described in Table 14.3.

It is critical, when doing a green tube alignment, that the linearity chart completely fill the active scan. To do this, zoom out until the vertical and horizontal edge markings can be seen. The center of the chart (marked by two connected circles) should be positioned in the center of the scan.

Electronic Deflection Adjustments

Shading

Shading adjustments are divided into two categories: static and dynamic.

Static shading is a correction made to the signal from the target. These correction signals are mixed with the individual tube channel output and fed to the video processing circuits. To maintain the non-uniformity of the target signal, these adjustments are performed with the lens capped. Otherwise, changes in the incoming video signal would distort the operator's ability to perceive the accuracy of

Table 14.3: Registering Green Tube Deflection

Camera Lens:	Set according to sensitivity specification.
Test Chart:	Ball Chart
Test Point:	Camera video output.
Test Equipment:	Black-and-white monitor for viewing camera output. Genlock sync generator with crosshatch pattern.
Procedure:	Run the camera video output through the sync generator's genlock input. This will cause the camera and sync generator to be synchronous. Input both the video from the camera output and the crosshatch pattern from the sync generator into the monitor. This can be accomplished with a barrel-T adaptor.
	Adjust the G size, centering and linearity controls so the crosspoints of the crosshatch signal fall in the center of the chart's circle.

Table 14.4: Procedure for Static Shading Adjustment

Test Equipment:	Oscilloscope
Equipment Setting:	Microsecond setting for horizontal adjustments. Millisecond setting for vertical adjustments.
Test Point:	Individual tube first stage processing outputs.
Controls:	Horizontal and vertical sawtooth and parabolic.
Procedure:	Adjust the sawtooth and parabolic controls in both the horizontal modes to obtain the flattest waveform.

Table 14.5: Dynamic Shading Adjustment Procedure

Test Equipment:	Oscilloscope or waveform monitor
Test Equipment Setting:	Oscilloscope: Millisecond setting with vertical sync for scope trigger. Waveform monitor: 2-volt setting.
Test Point:	Logarithmic gray scale or white card.
Lens Settings:	Set the lens to output a 100 IRE video signal.
Controls:	Horizontal and vertical sawtooth and parabolic.
Procedure:	Look at the highest part of the video signal and confirm that it is even from the beginning to the end of the vertical scan. Adjust the sawtooth and parabolic controls to obtain a flat waveform.

Table 14.6: Video Adjustments

Pre-amplifier

Lens Opening:	As per sensitivity specification.
Test Equipment:	Oscilloscope and video monitor.
Equipment Setting:	Oscilloscope: horizontal mode (20 microseconds)
Test Chart:	Depth of modulation, or line resolution chart.
Adjustments:	LF (low frequency); MF (medium frequency); HC (high frequency); Trimmer resistors
Procedure:	Low frequencies between 0.5 MHz to 1 MHz should be adjusted with the LF and MF trimmer resistors to have an amplitude of at least 0.6 volts video. (Remember that the setup pedestal level accounts for 0.1 volt.)
	The HF trimmer is set so that the highest frequency of 5 MHz has an amplitude equal to no less than 25% of the amplitude of the 5 MHz signal. The adjustment must be done so that the higher the frequency the lower the amplitude of each burst.

the adjustment. Table 14.4 states the procedure for making static shading adjustments with an oscilloscope.

While static shading corrects irregularities in the photoconductive area with no signal input, dynamic shading corrects irregularities in beam transmissions when the tube receives incoming light. Table 14.5 describes the procedure for dynamic shading adjustments.

Video Adjustments

Video adjustments are required so the camera will meet its specification for resolution. If adjustments are set too low, resolution will be lost; if adjustments are too high, the increased response over and above what the circuits can handle will cause streaking. Streaking (black streaks) is caused when the high frequency transitions between white and black shoot above the 100 IRE level and below the 0 IRE level and sync. Negative transitions can

cause the monitor to lose sync as it mistakes this negative video for sync. Table 14.6 lists the steps for making video adjustments.

White (Color) Balance Adjustments

Color balance adjustments achieve the unity of the three primary colors, which is necessary for a color camera to view white without any colorization (or, ''proper gray scale'').

Many three tube color cameras have both automatic and manual adjustments for achieving color balance. For automatic setups, the camera can be focused on any scene, provided it has a high degree of black and white contrast. Even when setting up the camera in the automatic mode, it is best to use a test chart that contains the black and white contrast ranges, which are within the limits of the television camera. As the auto black adjustment is performed with the iris closed, or with the lens capped, a white card may be substituted for

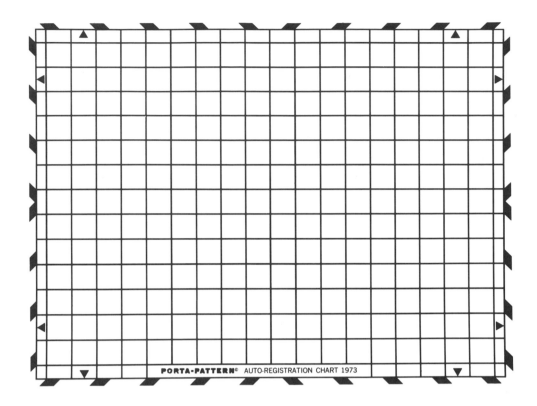

Figure 14.14: Auto-Registration Chart. Courtesy Porta-Pattern, Inc.

white setup when a test chart is unavailable. Even the registration chart contains enough white to be useful. (Figure 14.14 is a chart that can be used for auto-registration.)

After the camera is focused on the proper scene, auto color balance is accomplished by pressing a button or throwing a switch and holding it in place for approximately four to six seconds. This allows the camera microprocessor time to compare the incoming light with the levels that were preset during the complete camera setup performed under ideal conditions. The pedestal and white balance levels of red, blue and green are automatically set to achieve the best color balance. Even though these memorized settings can be held for long durations, auto white balance should be done prior to every new shoot, or when scene and/or lighting conditions are changed. Remember that changes in color temperature require the

operator to use the appropriate color filter prior to using auto color balance. If it is attempted with the incorrect color temperature filter, the resulting camera's color balance will be off and whites will look bluish or reddish.

Although automatic circuits are highly accurate, they are no substitute for a manual setup performed using the correct equipment. Table 14.7 describes the procedure for manual color balance adjustment. (Because color balance must be maintained at all video levels, each channel's gain must be set to the same value at each level of the video signal.)

ALIGNING THE SINGLE TUBE COLOR CAMERA

Single tube cameras are simpler to operate than three tube cameras because they do not require registration. Proper setup only calls for

Table 14.7: Color Balance Adjustment

Lens Opening:	To the f-stop in the sensitivity specification, or at the point where the video level is 0.7 volts.
Test Point:	Camera video output.
Test Equipment:	Waveform monitor.
Equipment Setting:	Sweep to 2H or 1H; Response: Flat
(Alternate Method):	
Test Equipment:	Vectorscope (Adjust the pedestal, gain and knee adjustments to the smallest center dot. Any signal leakage from the center point will result in chroma with a hue of the vector where the leakage occurs.)
Equipment Setting:	Gain to calibration.
Controls:	R-pedestal (black level) set to 7.5 IRE.
	G-pedestal (black level) set to 7.5 IRE.
	B-pedestal (black level) set to 7.5 IRE.
	R-gain (white level) set to 100 IRE.
	G-gain (white level) set to 100 IRE.
	B-gain (white level) set to 100 IRE.
	R-knee (waveform midpoint) approximately 0.58 IRE.
	G-knee (waveform midpoint) approximately 0.58 IRE.
	B-knee (waveform midpoint) approximately 0.58 IRE.
Procedure:	Adjust for minimum chroma at each step (level) of the gray scale. After performing this adjustment, iris down the lens and confirm that chroma does not leak into the signal. This is called color tracking. If chroma is present at lower video levels, re-do the adjustment.

adjusting the camera for proper color balance. Unlike the three tube color camera, the single tube camera has a two position filter switch instead of a color wheel. Settings are determined by the location of the shooting, either indoors or outdoors, and not by a specific color temperature.

As with the three tube camera, the quality of picture reproduction is dependent on the operation of the type of tube, and operation of the sync and deflection circuits. The single chip sync generator creates all the major pulses as in the three tube color camera. The horizontal and vertical deflection pulses are integrated into sawtooth waveforms and applied to the deflection yokes. The horizontal drive is coupled to the high voltage circuit and is used by the D.C.-to-D.C. converter to create the high voltage supply for the pickup tube. In

addition, the high voltage supply also powers the beam and target. Vertical and horizontal deflection pulses are changed into parabolic and sawtooth waveforms by a series of integrators for use in the camera's shading circuits.

The sync and deflection board also contains the encoder circuits, which use the subcarrier from the sync generator for R-y, B-y modulation.

Video Processing

The signal from the target output enters the preamplifier and is amplified by a series of transistors, beginning with an FET amplifier. The weak signal from the pickup tube must be amplified with a consideration to maintaining a high degree of signal-to-noise ratio. From the preamplifier, additional signal processing results in lowering the overall signal-to-noise

Figure 14.15: Window (or white) Chart. Courtesy Porta-Pattern, Inc.

Figure 14.16: Full-Field Color Bar Chart. Courtesy Porta-Pattern, Inc.

ratio because the video processing circuits add noise. Usually, in order to maintain a good signal-to-noise ratio, the last transistor amplifier is fed back to the first stage FET. This results in a better condition for signal transfer, and an improved frequency response.

For the three tube color camera, the primary consideration for frequency response centers around depth of modulation. In the single tube camera, the frequency response of the preamplifier directly affects color reproduction. Remember that the beam scanning across the stripe filter will produce a carrier frequency. This frequency will then be used to create red, green and blue. The frequency response of the preamplifier must remain flat safely past the point of the carrier frequency.

After the signal enters the video processing board from the preamplifier, the signal is D.C. clamped and amplified via an automatic gain control. The signal is then divided by means of lowpass and bandpass filter systems. The lowpass filter blocks the color carrier and allows the luminance (YH) signal to pass. The YH signal contains all the picture details; after passing through an additional low pass filter, a cut off point of 0.5 MHz is used to create the YL or green component.

The red and blue components are separated from the luminance carrier by means of a bandpass filter, whose center frequency is equal to the carrier created by the horizontal scan and dichroic stripe. Like the luminance signal, the color carrier is further separated into its red and blue components. This is accomplished by taking advantage of the 90° phase difference between the two colors created by the different angles of the cyan and yellow filters. The red and blue carriers are then added to the green (YL) signal, to form the R-y, B-y signal input for the NTSC encoder.

Camera Adjustments

Adjustment procedures begin by creating the right conditions. Allow the camera to warm up for at least 20 minutes.

Adjust the 3200° Kelvin lights to the lux or footcandle level, as indicated by the sensitivity specification in the manufacturer's service manual. Set the camera's filter or color control switch to 3200° Kelvin light. Open the camera's lens to the setting indicated by the camera's sensitivity specification (usually f-4 or f-5.6), or as indicated by the manufacturer's service manual.

Have the proper test charts available. For the single tube camera, adjustments will use the logarithmic gray scale (refer to Figure 14.9), a white card and a chart to check color reproduction (see Figures 14.15 and 14.16). Most manufacturer's provide a test chart with the camera to test color reproduction.

A registration chart is not necessary because single tube cameras do not require registration. In addition, geometric distortion will be determined by the setting of the beam deflection to obtain the best possible stripe filter output. You will have to live with any geometric distortion after the scan is set up. Many technicians have attempted to use the registration chart to set geometry and have been left frustrated, wondering why color reproduction is poor. Table 14.8 lists the adjustments for single tube camera setup.

You will notice that the average single tube camera does not have the variety of adjustments offered by the three tube camera. "Industrial" single tube cameras will distinguish themselves from "consumer" versions by having adjustable blanking. Most consumer model cameras have fixed output sync generators with no adjustments.

Horizontal Size and Linearity

A critical adjustment for color reproduction is horizontal size and linearity. The beam scan across the dichroic stripe must produce the exact carrier color frequency throughout the entire horizontal scan. Distortion at any point in the scan will cause the carrier to leak into the Yh (luminance signal) and reduce the amplitude of the red and blue signals. As a

(Continues on page 169.)

Table 14.8: Single Tube Camera Adjustments

SYNC GENERATOR ADJUSTMENTS

Test Point:	Camera video output
Test Condition:	Camera set to color bars. If your camera does not have an internal color bar generator, focus the camera on any stable scene, such as a test chart.
Test Equipment:	Waveform monitor.
Equipment Setting:	Response to IRE
	Sweep: 2H or 1H

Adjustment	Setting or Check
Y Level (luminance level)	100 IRE or 0.714 volts peak to peak
Sync Level	40 IRE or 0.286 volts peak to peak
Setup Level (black level or pedestal level)	7.5 IRE or 0.53 volts peak to peak
Horizontal Blanking Width	Change waveform monitor setting: Sweep: 1 microsecond/division
H Blanking	Minimum setting to 10.8 microsecond
Breezeway	Change waveform monitor setting: Response: Flat, to view the 3.58 MHz subcarrier.
Breezeway (burst start)	Separation of 0.381 microsecond from the rise of H sync to the start of the first cycle of burst.
Vertical Blanking Width	Change waveform monitor setting: Sweep: 2V Mag. (magnified)
V Blanking	Set to a minimum of 19H lines (remember to count two equalization pulses at one horizontal line).

ENCODER ADJUSTMENTS

Test Point:	Video output
Test Condition:	Camera set to color bars
Test Equipment:	Waveform monitor
Equipment Setting:	Response: Flat
	Sweep: 2H

Adjustment	Setting or Check
Burst Gain	40 IRE or 0.286 volts peak to peak
Luminance Level	Set to 75% or 0.56 volts peak to peak
Y Adjustment	Remember that R-y, B-y color bar generators (75% color bars) have an encoded white level of only 75% units.
Red and Blue White Balance	Adjust for minimum carrier in the white bar.
Red and Blue Carrier Balance	Adjust for minimum carrier at the pedestal and blanking levels.

Table 14.8: Single Tube Camera Adjustments (Cont.)

BURST PHASE AND CHROMA GAIN

Test Point: Video output
Test Condition: Color bars
Test Equipment: Vectorscope
Equipment Setting: Gain set to 75%

Adjustment   Setting or Check

Color Bar Phase   Adjust these three controls so the burst aligns with the vectorscope's
B-y Gain   burst axis and all the vectors fall into their respective boxes.
Color Bar Chroma
Gain

(Alternate Method):
When the camera does not have an internal color bar generator, perform the burst phase and chroma gain adjustments by focusing the camera on a flesh tone pattern (see Figure 14.17). Use the color monitor to judge the settings. To best use the color monitor as a test fixture, it must be preset with a color bar generator. Remember not to leave the monitor in the preset condition.

Adjustment   Setting or Check

Chroma Gain   Adjust for a reasonable color level.
Burst Phase   Adjust to obtain the best color reproduction.

DEFLECTION ADJUSTMENTS

(Note: Prior to making any electronic adjustments, preset all operator controls to their center positions and recheck the electronic color balance setting for 3200° Kelvin.)

Lens Setup: Set to f-4
Test Chart: White card (See Figure 14.18.)
Test Point: Output of blue processing amplifier.
Test Equipment: Oscilloscope
Equipment Setting: H rate: 10 or 20 microseconds per division

Adjustment   Setting or Check

(Note: Preset all static shading (dark shading) and all dynamic shading (target shading) adjustment controls to their mechanical centers.)

Electronic Focus   Adjust to obtain the maximum signal. As blue is the hardest signal for the
  (preliminary only)   stripe to produce, maximum blue is equal to the maximum filter output.

Table 14.8: Single Tube Camera Adjustments (Cont.)

TARGET VOLTAGE SETTING

Camera Condition:	Lens capped
Test Point:	Output of target voltage amplifier or lead to target.
Test Equipment:	Oscilloscope or digital voltmeter.
Equipment Setting:	Input to D.C. channel gain set to 10 volts per division.

Adjustment	Setting or Check
Target:	Manufacturer's specification as noted in the service manual.

BEAM

Camera Condition:	Lens set for largest opening or smallest f-stop number.
Test Chart:	Gray scale
Test Equipment:	Oscilloscope
Equipment Setting:	H rate 10 microseconds per division

Adjustment	Setting or Check
Beam:	Adjust the beam so that each of the levels of the gray scale can be seen.

DEFLECTION MAGNETIC ADJUSTMENTS

Camera Condition:	Lens set to f-4
Test Chart:	White card
Test Point:	Output of blue processing amplifier
Test Equipment:	Oscilloscope
Equipment Setting:	H rate 10 microseconds or 20 microseconds per division.

Adjustment	Setting or Check
Deflection Magnets	Rotate the magnets until the blue signal at the center of the horizontal scan is maximized. When this is done, the beam strikes the target at a 90° angle and maximum stripe filter resolution results in yielding maximum signal output.

TUBE ROTATION

(Note: The beam must cross the stripes to clearly define yellow, clear and cyan. The angle of intersection must therefore yield maximum filter resolution. Because each stripe is different, the response will not be completely flat, causing the output of each stripe to vary somewhat.)

Test Equipment Setting:	Place the oscilloscope in the V rate (approximately 2 microsecond) mode and use the delayed sweep to locate the center of the vertical scan. Switch the horizontal sweep rate to 20 microseconds.

Adjustment	Setting or Check
	Loosen the tube holding the screws located on the yoke assembly. Hold the tube socket (exercise caution as the socket can contain voltages as high as 1000 + volts D.C.) Rotate the tube for the flattest waveform.

Table 14.8: Single Tube Camera Adjustments (Cont.)

BACK FOCUS

(Note: When performing this adjustment, be careful not to loosen the tube set screw. Some back focus can be achieved by repositioning the tube itself. If the tube is repositioned, take care not to pull the tube backwards too far. When this occurs, the target contact between the yoke and tube can be broken. This can result in loss of picture. Prior to tightening the yoke set screw, make sure to check the tube rotation.)

Camera Condition:	Lens at widest opening (smallest f-stop number.)
Test Point:	Video output
Test Equipment:	Black-and-white or color monitor. If you use a color monitor, make sure you turn the color off.
Test Chart:	Registration chart or any chart with fine details.

Adjustment	Setting or Check
Back Focus Screw:	Loosen the coil assembly screws. Zoom in the lens and adjust for the best focus. Zoom out and adjust the back focus screw for the best focus. Zoom the lens in and check for focus with the zoom lens set at closeup, medium range and telephoto. Best focus should be obtained at each point without having to re-adjust the lens focus.

Table 14.9: Horizontal Size and Linearity Adjustments

Camera Condition:	Lens opened to f-4.
Test Point:	Output of LPF for the YH signal or output of BPF for chroma signal.
Test Equipment:	Oscilloscope set to horizontal 10 microsecond rate.
Equipment Setting:	Main time base set to 10 microseconds per division. Delay sweep set to 2 microseconds per division.

Adjustment	Setting or Check
Horizontal Size:	Locate the center of the horizontal line and adjust the sine wave for a 0.25 microsecond duration. When viewing the output of the BPF, adjust for maximum amplitude at the center of the waveform. When viewing the output of the LPF, adjust for minimum amplitude at the center of the waveform.
Horizontal Linearity Lin-1, Lin-2	Locate the start of the horizontal line and use the delay mode to observe the individual sine wave. Adjust the corresponding linearity control for a 0.25 microsecond duration. When viewing the output of the BPF, adjust for maximum amplitude at the beginning of the horizontal line. When viewing the output of the LPF, adjust for minimum amplitude at the end of the waveform.

Figure 14.17: Flesh Tone Reference Test Card. Courtesy Porta-Pattern, Inc.

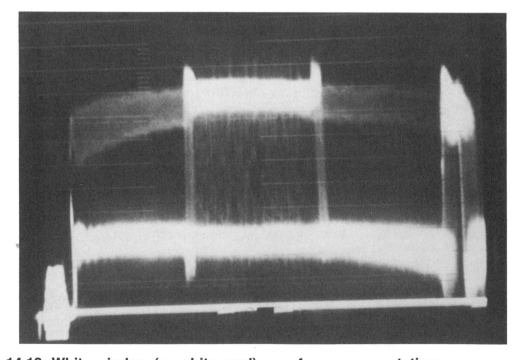

Figure 14.18: White window (or white card) waveform representation.

result, it will not be possible to achieve unity of the three primaries in that part of the picture. In most cases, the base color of green will prevail, and the picture will take on a green or greenish-yellow hue.

To make this adjustment, you must first calculate the duration of the carrier sine wave. This can be done by dividing the stripe filter as specified by the manufacturer into one, which results in the time period of the carrier frequency. For example, let's assume that the camera in question has a 3.8 MHz carrier. The period would be 1/3.8 MHz, or 0.25 microseconds. The delay mode of the scope can be used to view this signal.

Table 14.9 lists the steps for horizontal size and linearity adjustments.

Vertical Size and Linearity

In setting the horizontal scan, we established a consistent carrier frequency for each horizontal line. Even though the vertical scan is made up of horizontal lines, we must still adjust the vertical scanning so the frequency is maintained for each field. When the horizontal and vertical scans are properly adjusted, the result-

ing frequency will be that of the carrier. We will call this the zero frequency. When the rate of the vertical scan is offset, the rate of the carrier is changed at that particular point (top, middle or bottom of the picture). In electronics, when two frequencies that are equal are slightly offset, they beat. The further apart they are from each other, the more they beat. The closer they are, the less they beat. And when they are the same, no beating, or "zero beating" occurs. The adjustments for vertical size and linearity are described in Table 14.10.

Centering Adjustments

In addition to the dichroic filter, the target faceplate contains an optical black stripe. During each horizontal line, the beam scans across this black stripe, creating a D.C. level that becomes the camera pedestal or black level. The horizontal or clamping adjustment provides room within the H scan for this black stripe.

In some cameras, horizontal centering is the same as horizontal size. When this is the case, refer to horizontal size for this adjustment procedure, plus recheck the beam and focus. Table

Table 14.10: Vertical Size and Linearity Adjustments

Test Point: Video output, or the output of either the red or blue processors.
Test Equipment: Oscilloscope
Equipment Setting: Vertical rate milliseconds

Adjustment   Setting or Check

Vertical Size   Adjust for zero beat at the center of the scan.
Vertical Linearity   Adjust for zero beat at the ends of the vertical scan.

Table 14.11: Centering Adjustments

HORIZONTAL CENTERING OR BLACK CLAMP ADJUSTMENT

Test Chart: White card
Test Point: Output of preamplifier
Test Equipment: Oscilloscope
Equipment Setting: 1 microsecond per division

Adjustment   Setting or Check

H Centering:
H Clamp: Adjust for the duration from the end of the horizontal scan as indicated by
  (optical black)   the service manual. The clamping width is usually between 2 to
                       4 microseconds.

VERTICAL CENTERING ADJUSTMENT

Test Chart: White card. Place a marker in the center of the chart with enough contrast
                       to result in change of voltage at the center point of the vertical scan.

Adjustment   Setting or Check

Vertical Centering   Adjust the vertical centering so the marker appears in the exact center
                       of the vertical scan.

Table 14.12: Dynamic Focus

Camera Condition: Lens set at f-4 or f-5.6.
Test Point: Video preamplifier output or the output of the individual red, green and
                       blue channel outputs.
Test Chart: White card
Test Equipment: Color monitor and oscilloscope
Equipment Setting: Oscilloscope set to H rate, 20 microseconds per division.

Adjustment   Setting or Check

H Parabolic   When using the video monitor: adjust for minimum green in the picture
V Parabolic   edges.
H Sawtooth   When using the oscilloscope, adjust for the flattest signal in the vertical
V Sawtooth   and horizontal rates.

Table 14.13: Red and Blue Separation Adjustments

Camera Condition:	Lens set to f-4
Test Chart:	Gray scale, Test Points: Channel one: output of red signal processor.
	Channel two: output of blue signal processor.
Test Equipment:	Oscilloscope
Equipment Setting:	H rate 20 microseconds per division; dual trace mode.

Adjustment	Setting or Check
R/B Separation	Adjust for the maximum amplitude and least contamination for each signal output.

Table 14.14: White Balance Adjustments

Camera Condition:	Lens set to sensitivity specification to create a 0.7 output.
Test Point:	Final output of each of the red, green and blue channels.
Test Equipment:	Oscilloscope
Equipment Setting:	Sweep: 20 microseconds per division.
	Amplitude: 0.1 volt per division.

Adjustment	Setting or Check
Yellow Pedestal	
Red Pedestal	
Green Pedestal	Adjust for a DC pedestal setting of 0.1 volts.
Yellow Gain	
Red Gain	
Blue Gain	Adjust for a D.C. gain of 0.7 volts of video.
Yellow Tracking	
Red Tracking	
Blue Tracking	Adjust for the level as indicated by the manufacturer's service manual.

Alternate Method (A):

Test Output:	Camera video output
Test Equipment:	Waveform monitor
Equipment Setting:	Response: Flat
	Sweep: 2H

Adjustment	Setting or Check
Yellow Pedestal	
Red Pedestal	
Blue Pedestal	Adjust for minimum chroma at the pedestal level.
Yellow Gain	
Red Gain	
Blue Gain	Adjust for minimum chroma at the top of the waveform.
Yellow Tracking	
Red Tracking	

Table 14.14: White Balance Adjustments (Cont.)

Blue Tracking	Adjust for minimum chroma at the center of the waveform. (Confirm tracking adjustments by slowly closing the lens and looking for chroma in the waveform. White balance must be maintained with changes in incoming light.)

Alternate Method (B):

Test Output:	Camera video output
Test Equipment:	Vectorscope
Equipment Setting:	Gain at calibration

Adjustment	Setting or Check
Yellow Gain	
Red Gain	
Blue Gain	Adjust for minimum subcarrier leakage and for the smallest center dot on the vectorscope.
Yellow Pedestal	
Red Pedestal	
Blue Pedestal	Adjust for minimum subcarrier leakage and for the smallest center dot
Yellow Tracking	on the vectorscope.
Red Tracking	
Blue Tracking	Adjust for minimum subcarrier leakage and for the smallest center dot on the vectorscope.

Figure 14.19: Cameras used within systems.

Table 14.15: Gen Lock Circuit Adjustments

Test Conditions:	Input a color signal to the gen lock input of the camera.
Test Equipment:	Oscilloscope
Channel one:	Gen lock signal input.
Channel two:	Composite output of camera's internal sync generator.
Equipment Setting:	20 microseconds per division.

Adjustment	Setting or Check
H Phase	Adjust so that the falling edge of the H syncs are aligned.

(Alternate Method):

Equipment Setting:	Use the delay mode to look at the burst of each signal.

Adjustment	Setting or Check
S.C. Phase	Adjust the subcarrier phase to have the same phase.

Alternate Method (Visual):

Test Condition:	Input the camera signals into a television production switcher. The switcher and camera must be synced for the same reference video or black burst.
Camera Condition:	Set the camera to color bars
Test Equipment:	Color monitor viewing the output of the video switcher

Adjustment	Setting or Check
H Phase	Set up a vertical wipe between each of the cameras and system bars. As the wipe reaches the limit of each of the switch points, the reference between the first camera and the system bars will cause a difference in H phase to show up as horizontal movement. Continue to switch between the two signals and adjust the H phase until the H shift is minimized.
S.C. Phase	Adjust the hue of the monitor using the system color bars to obtain the best yellow hue. Follow procedures for adjusting H phase. This time adjust for any hue shifts as the switcher handle moves between the upper and lower limits.

14.11 describes the procedures for adjusting horizontal centering as well as vertical centering.

Dynamic Focus

Dynamic focus (or shading) compensates for distortion on the target faceplate. The monitor is used as a test fixture. Check your camera before attempting this adjustment; some "industrial" single tube cameras have dynamic shading adjustments for the individual red, green and blue signals. (See Table 14.12.)

Red and Blue Separation Adjustments

After the signal from the preamplifier passes through the BPF, the red and blue color signals need to be separated. The total color signal is a combination of two horizontal lines. To separate the colors, the camera electronics must shift the signal 90° to match the phase shift created by the physical layout of the dichroic stripes. By adjusting the R/B separation, we electronically adjust the 90° phase shift, thereby regulating the amount of red/blue separation.

The steps outlined in Table 14.13 describe the procedure to create separate red, green and blue signals, as well as a luminance component that contains the picture details. The adjustments made to the single tube camera from this point on match those for the three tube camera to create a unity of white balance. (See Table 14.14.)

CAMERAS WITHIN SYSTEMS

Cameras can be used alone (ENG/EFP) or in groups (TV and production use; see Figure 14.19). When a camera is used alone, the setup procedure is simple because it is the only source feeding the videotape recorder. In multicamera setups, each camera *must* be perfectly synchronized with regard to the vertical sync rate, horizontal sync rate and the phase of the color subcarrier.

In the following section we will examine the adjustments required for cameras operating as part of a group. (Presently, only professional or industrial cameras are capable of operation within a system.)

Referencing to the Burst Signal

Television systems using more than one camera must be made to reference to the same sync and burst phase. The synchronous reference in a multiple camera system must come from one source. In its simplest form, the reference is taken from the switcher, which usually contains an internal sync generator.

To simplify the system hookup, all signals needed to "sync" a camera can be carried by a single signal source—black burst. The black burst signal contains all the components of a complete video signal: horizontal and vertical sync (composite sync); color burst; and active video (7.5 IRE pedestal level).

Cameras are able to receive and reference to the black burst signal with a gen lock. Gen lock is a circuit that strips away the sync and burst components and compares them to the camera's internal generator. Minor differences between the two signals can be adjusted through operator controls—subcarrier and horizontal phase. The composite video signal or black burst signal enters the camera's gen lock input. The 3.58 MHz component (burst and chroma) are stripped away by means of a high pass filter. The remaining composite sync signal is further separated into its vertical and horizontal parts by additional filtering systems. The external vertical drive is used to reset the timing of the camera's internal sync. The separated horizontal sync is used for two purposes: First, it is delayed and made to coincide with the timing of the burst. This burst gate pulse is used to confirm that the external signal being compared to the internal signal is color. The external burst is then compared in the internal generator. The internal generator, a voltage controlled oscillator (VCO), outputs a frequency according to its input voltage. The difference in phase between the gen lock burst and the VCO burst results in a correction voltage, which adjusts the frequency (phase) to that of the input (genlock) signal. If two cameras in a system have the same phase as the reference sync generator, they are in sync.

Horizontal Sync Phase

Gen-locking to the external horizontal (H) signals operates in a similar way as gen-locking to the burst signal.

The external and internal H signals are compared to each other in a phase detector. The error voltage then regulates a VCO frequency. For horizontal sync phase control, the actual VCO is usually a high frequency multiple of the H frequency. This is due to the difficulty in operating VCO's at such low frequencies. (15.75 KHZ)

Table 14.15 describes the procedure for making gen lock circuit adjustments. This procedure should be repeated for each camera in the system.

CONCLUSION

In this chapter we have reviewed the procedures for camera alignment and setup. In Chapter 15 we will continue our discussion of camera setup with relation to features available on various models, as well as camera operation.

15 Getting the Most Out of Your Camera

With few exceptions, color cameras are almost 100% solid state. Solid state components usually operate reliably for many years. The main component of the color camera, the image pickup tube, is a thermeonic device. As such, the combination of incoming light and beam projection can burn off large areas of the target faceplate. For this reason, the life of the camera is directly related to the operation time of its tube(s).

CHANGING TUBES: WHEN AND WHY

Tube changes usually require a complete camera realignment. Replacement tubes are expensive, and the cost of labor can at times be more expensive than the tube itself. The decision to replace a camera tube, therefore, should be based on one of two factors: tube aging, or tube damage.

Tube Aging

When a tube ages its target burns off. When this occurs, the dark current increases (see Figure 15.1), accompanied by the related symptoms of reduced contrast, reduced signal-to-noise ratio, reduced resolution and increased lag.

Due to their high sensitivity specifications and lack of a stripe filter, three tube color cameras have an advantage in operating life over single tube cameras. Deterioration of the target faceplate in a single tube camera causes loss of resolution of stripe dichroics. When this happens, the camera loses its ability to produce red and blue. The signal left yields green. This loss is not limited to the faceplate. Differences in beam scanning can also be caused by misalignment of the yoke assembly. Continuous uneven beam scan across the target faceplate can cause some areas to burn off faster than others. When this happens, the single tube camera develops patches of green.

Tube Damage

Tube damage is one of those conditions in which good judgement and proper handling can go a long way to preventing costly repairs. The most common type of tube damage is caused by the inexperienced operator, who

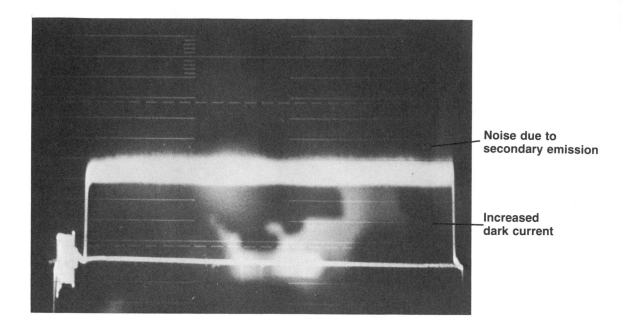

Figure 15.1: Increased dark current caused by aging tube.

mistakenly points his or her camera at the sun or a high contrast scene. Concentrated light decreases the variable properties of the target to the point where it can no longer respond to changing light levels. Usually, the damage is confined to a spot on the faceplate, rather than the entire faceplate. There are myths that certain types of tubes cannot be burnt. This is not true because targets are subject to burns—the target material determines the degree of susceptibility. Burn damage can occur even when the camera is not operational. Always remember to iris down and cap the camera lens when the camera is not in use.

Dust

Do not make the costly mistake of confusing burns with dust. Burns show up as white spots because of the absence of target material. Dust reduces the amount of light available to the target and shows up as gray spots, which vary in contrast as the lens is opened and closed.

In addition, as the dust particles lie on top of the target's focal plane, they will appear slightly out of focus. If you think you have a dust problem, carefully clean the lens glass and optical faceplate with a non-abrasive tissue. If this does not solve the problem, remove the tube from the yoke assembly and clean the target faceplate. Remember, if you remove the tube, the camera must be re-setup to get it into operating condition.

Spotting

Similar to tube burning is tube spotting. Never leave the camera resting on its lens. Because of the construction of the image pickup tube, bits of metallic dust have a tendency to adhere to the positive potential of the target faceplate. These metal particles can physically punch holes in the target or alter the ability of the tube to produce proper pictures. It is, therefore, advisable to avoid holding the camera in

Figure 15.2: Holding the camera.

(a.) Improper camera position.

(b.) Proper camera position.

ways that might allow gravity to aggravate this condition. Never hold the camera with the lens pointing down. (See Figure 15.2.) If the camera is resting on a tripod, leave it tilted up at a slight angle.

Temperature

Avoid placing the camera in high temperature situations. We all want to keep video equipment in safe places, however, leaving your camera in the back seat of a car or in the trunk are good ways to damage the tube. High temperatures (above 104° F or 40° C) can break down the chemical structure of the tube and lower the target resistance. This can cause an image to easily burn into the faceplate. You can attempt to correct this condition by defocusing your camera on a well-lit white background. This method of rejuvenating the tube is often used on black-and-white cameras. However, due to the operation of the color camera tube, the sensitivity may be reduced to a point where it can no longer produce color, or the picture may be too noisy. If you want to try rejuvenating the tube, make sure that the lens opening is no greater than f−4. If you run your camera this way for approximately one to two hours, the image should "burn out." Be prepared, however, to accept the fact that even though this method may succeed in giving you an acceptable picture, the tube will still need to be replaced because its life will have been substantially shortened.

CHANGING TUBES

Before beginning any disassembly procedure, make sure the camera power is off.

First, open the camera's outer casing and remove the plug in the circuit boards to expose the optical block assembly. At this point, the type of camera assembly you have can be clearly identified—tubes positioned parallel to each other comprise a mirror system; tubes positioned at a 45° angle to the center tube make up a prism optical system. (See Figure 15.3.)

Follow the steps outlined below to remove tubes:

1. Locate the tube's power socket at the rear of the tube and remove it.
2. Locate a disk at the center of each of the tube assemblies. This houses the tube rotation and back focus mechanism. Remove the set screws and then the mechanism itself.
3. Loosen the yoke lock screw and remove the deflection yoke from the optical block. In some cases, the yoke is part of the optical block. Loosening the setscrew in this case will allow you to remove the tube.
4. When the yoke and tube assemblies must be removed together, the tube is usually held in place by a collar or locking ring. Locate the locking mechanism and pull the tube straight back. Be careful not to turn or twist the tube as it can damage the target and target contact. (See Figure 15.4.)

Inserting the New Pickup Tube

When replacing camera tubes, confirm that the replacement tube you are using is recommended by the manufacturer. Different types of tubes are not interchangeable. Only in certain cases can a camera containing Pbo tubes be reconfigured to accommodate Saticon tubes. Be sure to work in a clean, controlled environment. Never attempt to change tubes outdoors. Not only is dirt a problem, but direct sunlight can damage the tube's target. Take care in handling the tube. Any strong shock will damage the tube. Do not touch the faceplate directly with your fingers. If you must contact the target, use a lens tissue. If the target becomes subject to finger prints or dirt, use an alcohol ethyl mixture to remove the foreign matter.

Prior to inserting the pickup tube, make sure

Figure 15.3: Tubes positioned in camera using prism optical system.

(a.) Exposed block displaying tubes.

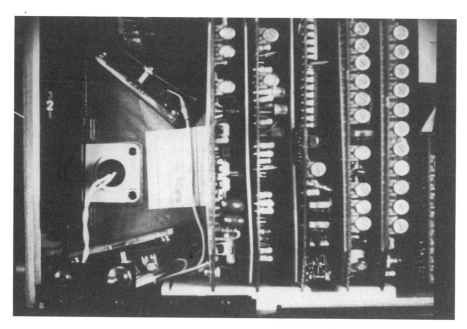

(b.) Block displaying chips.

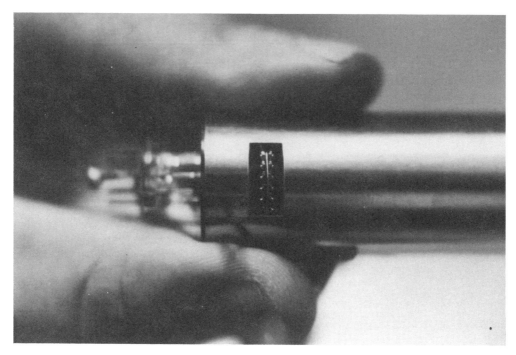

Figure 15.4: Tube in yoke assembly.

that the target faceplate is clean, then proceed as detailed below:

1. Set the tube in the yoke so the target pin of the tube makes contact with the target and the yoke. If the contact leads are not aligned, do not attempt to twist the tube in the yoke. Remove the tube and reinsert it.

2. Once the tube is firmly seated in the yoke, look at the front of the yoke assembly to confirm that the scanning area of the tube is parallel to the deflection yoke. The physical alignment between the tube and yoke is critical to proper electronic operation. During scanning, the beam must intersect the faceplate at vertical and horizontal perpendicular angles to the 3 by 4 target area. Mispositioning of the tube will cause the beam to scan areas other than the target, which results in incomplete picture scan and tilted picture reproduction.

3. As noted before, in some three tube cameras, the deflection yoke is part of the optical block assembly. On these cameras, the tube is pulled from and then inserted into the yoke assembly/optical block. Since it is impossible to judge target alignment by looking at the front of the yoke assembly, this adjustment must be done by viewing the back end of the tube, which contains the pins that connect the tube to the tube socket. All tubes have one pin cut short or missing—the key pin. Check the manufacturer's manual for the correct positioning of the key pin to ensure that the scanning area will be properly aligned.

Possible Problems

After the tube changes are complete, and all connections have been firmly made, turn the camera on to confirm proper operation. If there is no output from a particular channel, it is possible that the yoke and target connects are not aligned.

Check the output of the channel by connecting a scope probe to the first stage amplifier after the pre-amplifier. If no signal is present, turn the camera off and repeat the tube changing process. This time, carefully check the faceplate or key pin alignment. Remember—avoid the urge to twist the tube while it is in the yoke.

For instructions on camera alignment procedures (which must be performed after tube replacement), refer to Chapter 14.

Part 3
Appendices

Appendix A: Videotape Recorder Specifications

Power Source: The power source defines the amount of power needed to operate a recorder. Power is expressed as either volts (V) and amperes (amps) or watts, which is a product of both. The electronic equation for power is:

$$P(watts) = E(voltage) \times I (amperage)$$

Recorders that use power from wall outlets usually require standard A.C. (alternating current) power which is 120V at 20 amps.

Portable recorders depend on the power of a battery source, and the length of time the recorder will play depends on the power rating of that battery source. To calculate the total operation time of your field equipment, you must determine its total power consumption. For portable equipment, we can make a fair assumption that the supply voltage will be 12v. The recorder's specification sheet will express the power requirements of the recorder either in watts or amps. If the specification given is in amps, you multiply the number by 12 (volts) to obtain the power figure. If the specification is given as watts or power, you divide that number by 12 to obtain the amperage.

Whether you use watts or amps is determined by the way power is expressed on the battery. Most portable power sources are rated in terms of amp-hours. For example, a battery rated at five amp-hours will produce one amp for a period of five hours, or two-and-a-half amps for a period of two hours.

When using a single power source such as a battery pack to power both a camera and portable videotape recorder, it is necessary to add together the power consumption of both the camera and the recorder. (I recommend taking 80% of the sum to ensure against unreliable operation under low power.) The resulting sum can be used to determine the number of fully charged spare batteries you will require to see you through hours of field production.

When purchasing an A.C. power supply and battery charge for your portable equipment, the power specification should also be taken into consideration. Portable video equipment that requires 12V direct current is blind to the phase and voltage of the power provided by A.C. wall outlets. And, if a possibility exists that you will be shooting video in a foreign country, you should select a power supply/battery charger that is capable of handling 50 Hz 220V power sources.

Television System: This specification identifies the type of television system with which a recorder is compatible. In the United States, the Electronic Industry Association (EIA) standard represents the 525 television line, 60 fields per second system. This standard, however, offers no specifications for color and is usually followed by a specification created by the National Television Standards Committee (NTSC), which defines the standard United States color television signal.

Some videotape recorders are able to record and playback multiple types of color television signals, besides NTSC. These television systems include Phase Alternating Line (PAL), the color system primarily found in Europe; SECAM, used in France and Russia; and a modified NTSC system, which uses the 4.43 color subcarrier found in the PAL television system.

A recorder's television system specification will also list the standard system it can record and playback. Do not mistake this specification as an indication that the recorder can record one television system standard and playback in another. The standard used to playback a tape must be the same as the one in which the tape was recorded.

Video Recording System: This specification is broken down into components that specify the number of recording heads on the recorder and the various methods of recording that can be employed.

A "rotary recording system" indicates that the video heads are mounted on a rotating upper drum cylinder and that a recording is produced by the spinning heads contacting the tape. On VHS, Beta and 3/4-inch standard recorders, where each head records one field of video, the recording and playback processes are accomplished by two video heads. For these recorders the specifications will read "two head rotary record system." For other types of recording systems, where signals are segregated into different signal components, the specification will indicate the number of heads used to record a complete frame of video. For example, the M format specification would read "rotary head system with separate recording heads of luminance, I and Q."

The next part of this specification defines the state of the signal when it is recorded on the tape. Frequency modulated luminance and converted subcarrier are specifications for 3/4-inch and 1/2-inch videotape recorder systems. In these recorders, the recording bandwidth limitation requires that the incoming video signal be converted to a smaller bandwidth.

A direct recording specification indicates that all the frequencies present in the original video signal will be recorded directly on the tape. It refers to the frequencies found in standard baseband television signals. The video luminance signal is present between 0 MHz to 4.2 MHz and the color burst signal is at 3.58 MHz.

Resolution: Resolution is the amount and degree of detail in the video image. Different recording methods result in different resolutions. *Converted signals* limit the bandwidth of the recorded signal and thereby limit the amount of recorded resolution. Converted frequency recording resolution is measured against a test pattern on a monitor. The upper limit of horizontal resolution is determined by the point at which the individual lines blend together. This method, known as "limiting resolution," depends on the judgment of the human eye. Because everyone's "judgment" is not the same, this specification is often written as being "greater than" a particular number of horizontal lines.

Direct recording systems must be able to handle the resolution contained within the full video bandwidth (0 MHz to 4.2 MHz). Specifications for direct recording systems, therefore, measure resolution in terms of signal loss at the highest recorded frequency of 4.2 MHz compared to the lowest recorded frequency of 0.5 MHz.

The key measurement for video is taken in volts; however, to understand resolution you must first understand the decibel (db). The decibel measures signal strength on a logarithmic scale. A loss of 3db is a signal loss of approximately 30%. A loss of 6db is a signal loss of approximately 50%. The standard cut-off point for bandwidth signal measurement is the point at which the signal drops below 3db. A typical resolution specification for a SMPTE type C recorder, for example, would read 4.2 MHz − 3db. Since greater bandwidth equals higher resolution, the same amount of signal loss at a lower frequency would represent a greater loss of resolution.

When reading the resolution specification for *converted subcarrier recorders,* the filtering system used to accommodate color limits the resolution of the color playback signal.

Signal-to-Noise Ratio: This specification measures the amount of noise contained within the video signal. The greater the amount (or intensity) of noise, the poorer the quality of the playback picture. Signal-to-noise is a ratio that measures the intensity of the video signal compared to the noise. The measurement is expressed in decibels, with the signal noise set at a zero decibel reference. Typical measurements range between 40 db to 45 db for 1/2-inch VHS, Beta, and 3/4-inch recorders. Broadcast recorders typically have signal-to-noise specifications of 35db and above.

When reading signal-to-noise specifications, there are two important factors to keep in mind. First, unless otherwise indicated, the specification is taken in the black and white playback mode. Playback in the color mode increases the noise factor as the signal is passed through the additional color processing circuits. The color playback picture you view has a lower signal-to-noise ratio specification than the one indicated on the specification sheet. The second factor to keep in mind is that more signal is lost and more noise is gained each time a signal is copied. Recorders starting out with the highest amount of signal-to-noise ratio will have the best signal-to-noise after the editing and master processes.

The Audio Signal: (Frequency Response and Signal-to-Noise Ratio) Just as video specifications for frequency response and signal-to-noise ratio are important, so are those for the recorded audio signal. Frequency response is measured against the range of audible tones that are found between 15 cycles per second and 15,000 cycles per second. The greater the frequency response, the better the audio reproduction. Typical values set the upper limits of frequency response at 12,000 cycles per second for 1/2-inch consumer recorders and 15,000 cycles per second for "broadcast" type recorders. The lack of audio frequency and the associated decrease in signal-to-noise ratio are not as noticeable as are video losses.

Appendix B: Video Camera Specifications

Sensitivity: Sensitivity is defined by the lighting level and f-stop setting required to produced a 100% IRE video signal. This setting is used for all camera adjustments, and sets the conditions for determining other camera specifications. The lighting level is determined by setting the camera's lens at its midpoint f-stop, usually f-4. Using the lens' midpoint as a specification setting allows the camera to respond to the greatest number of high and low light conditions. As the f-stop is usually a standard setting, the amount of light becomes the determining factor of this specification. The lower the amount of light to produce a 100% IRE output, the better the camera's sensitivity. Prism tube cameras have the best sensitivity due to the light transfer characteristics of the prism system. Next is the three tube mirror camera, followed by the single tube camera.

Minimum Illumination: The minimum illumination specification indicates the lowest amount of light a camera can tolerate to produce a usable picture. To determine this specification, the camera's lens is set to its lowest f-stop setting (widest opening). All gain boosts are set to their highest positions and the light level is adjusted until the video output is 100 IRE. Remember that with the gain of the video signal boosted, the overall signal-to-noise ratio will drop considerably.

Signal-to-Noise Ratio: This is the ratio of useful video information to noise or snow within the television picture. Noise in a camera begins at the input to the pre-amplifier, when the signal is taken directly from the tube's faceplate and amplified. All stages following the pre-amplifier add to the camera's noise. Therefore, the rest of the camera video processing components must be selected for minimum noise output. In recent years, advances have been made to increase the signal-to-noise of field effect transistors (FET). As FETs serve as the signal input to the camera's pre-amplifier, if their signal-to-noise ratio increases, so does the camera's overall signal-to-noise ratio specification.

In measuring signal-to-noise ratio, the absolute unit is fixed at an arbitrary "zero" level. Relationships are either above (+) or below (−) this level. The decibel (db) scale is not a linear scale. Key figures to remember are losses of 3 db and 6 db. A 3 db loss is approximately a loss of 30% of signal compared to noise. A 6 db loss equals a loss of 50%. Signal-to-noise is important when considering the advantage of using the camera's gain boost under low light conditions. In addition, television signals lose signal-to-noise each time a recording is made. If you consider this to be a loss of approximately 3 db, a tape that is subject to both editing and duplication can lose more than half of its signal strength compared to noise. It is a matter of opinion when a tape is too noisy to be viewed. Studies have shown this figure to be about 28db.

Generally speaking, cameras should have signal-to-noise between 42 db and 45 db in order to be used for most types of shooting and post-production situations. When considering the signal-to-noise specification, it is important to note the conditions of the test. All enhancement video processing, such as I and Q are also turned off. As a result, the measurement reflects the complete video bandwidth to 4.2 MHz.

Horizontal Resolution: Television pictures are created by changes in voltage along the tube's target faceplate. Horizontal resolution is defined as the maximum number of voltage changes that occur as an individual line is scanned. These changes depend on the makeup of the target faceplate and definition of beam. In addition, regardless of the internal tube structure, the electronics of the camera's video processing section must be able to have a great enough bandwidth to pass these frequencies.

Ideally, the alternating black and white picture elements would produce a square wave. However, due to the bandwidth limitations of the camera electronics, the ideal square wave is reproduced as a sine wave. This causes the transition points of the square wave to blur. As the frequency of the black and white transitions increases, so does the camera's AC resistance (otherwise known as impedence). As a result, the higher the frequency of the picture elements, the more rounded the sine wave becomes, and the lower the amplitude. To the viewer, horizontal transitions become blurred and melt into a contrastless gray. In effect, resolution (detail) is lost.

Resolution in a camera can be measured in two different ways. One method—Depth of Modulation—is empirical; the other—limiting resolution—is a matter of the viewer's judgment.

Depth of Modulation—As the primary factor of camera resolution is the tube itself, depth of modulation measures the ability of the tube to react to changes in incoming light. This measurement is also known as the tube's modulation transfer function, or M.T.F. To measure this factor, we use a Depth of Modulation chart, which contains a set of black and white lines ranging in frequency from 0.5 MHz to 5 MHz. These bursts of frequency are positioned so they are scanned by the center of the tube. The upper limit of the camera's resolution is set at the point where the amplitude of a particular burst falls below 30% of the amplitude of the 0.5 MHz burst.

To determine the relationship of television lines to frequency, we consider the frequency of the picture elements. This is expressed as a period of time within the duration of the active scan:

$$\text{Active Video} = \text{One Horizontal Line} = \text{Blanking Period}$$
$$52.7 = 63.5 \text{ us} - 10.8 \text{ us}$$

$$\text{The period of 5 MHz} = 1/5,000,000 = 0.2 \text{ us}$$
$$\text{Television lines} = 52.7 \text{ us}/0.2 \text{ us} = 263.5.$$

The equation presented above represents one half of the cycle. As we are concerned with the transition from white to black, or the transition made by the interlaced picture, we must double this figure.

$$263.5 \times 2 = 527$$

Next, we consider the 3×4 aspect ratio of the television system. As television lines relate more to vertical than horizontal, the resulting figure is multiplied by 3/4, or

$$525 \times 3/4 = 392.5.$$

If we round this figure, to 400 TVL (television lines) and divide it by the frequency of the picture elements, we will find the number of television lines contained within 1 MHz—400/5 = 80 TVL.

This formula is open to some interpretation. At times, manufacturers may stretch 80 lines per MHz to 100 lines and drop the limiting percentage to 25% instead of 30%. For this reason, an exact specification of depth of modulation would indicate the number of lines measured at the percentage compared to 0.5 MHz.

Another important factor is the condition under which the resolution specification is determined.

Lens and Lighting—Changes in video level cause changes in overall picture contrast. Loss of contrast results in loss of detail. Resolution is determined by setting the lighting conditions of the sensitivity specification.

Color Wavelength—The green wavelength accounts for 59% of the detail of white light. Sensitivity falls off to 30% in the red component, and 11% in the blue component. For this reason, resolution of a three tube camera is taken from the output of the green channel.

Deflection—Regardless of the quality of the tube and yoke, resolution is best in the center of the tube and falls off in the target corners. Resolution is therefore measured at the center of the tube.

A more accurate resolution specification would now read:

600 lines at X% depth of modulation measured at center G (channel).

This is hardly the way we would typically operate our camera. For this reason, many operators choose to evaluate their cameras on the basis of limiting resolution. This method of resolution is taken from the camera's output. To determine limiting resolution, we focus the camera on a registration or resolution chart. The measurement is based on the highest frequency that the eye can see. This is the point where the individual lines can be seen prior to melting into solid black.

Since high frequency noise is low in signal amplitude, the human eye integrates it into the picture. As a result, limiting resolution is best viewed on a television monitor, which masks the noise, rather than on a waveform monitor, which does not. When using the limiting resolution method, remember that the resolution of the monitor must exceed the resolution of the camera.

Geometric Distortion: Geometric distortion is defined as any deviation which causes the reproduced picture to be dissimilar in ratio to the original image. This distortion is due to the inability of the beam to maintain consistency as it scans across the target faceplate. Bends in the scan cause the reproduced image to bend. As with picture resolution, geometric distortion is less in the center and increases towards the picture edges. To the viewer, geometric distortion can cause circular objects positioned in the corner of the frame to appear egg shaped.

Geometric distortion is measured with the registration chart. The active scan is divided into three areas, or zones:

Zone one is defined as 80% or less of the picture height.

Zone two is defined as a circle with the height equal to that of the picture.

Zone three is the remaining area outside of zone two.

Distortion within zone one is usually about 1%, while zones two and three can range between 2% and 3%.

In a three tube camera, each one of the three individual yokes yields distortion figures that are slightly different from each other. As a result absolute matched registration is not possible. Like geometric distortion, registration "errors" are measured by zones. Most cameras have a zone one error of 0.1%. Differences in the quality of yokes and tubes show up as we move into zone two and three, where registration error increases. For zone two, errors are usually 0.2% to 0.4%, while zone three errors range between 0.4% and 0.8%, depending on the quality of the yoke and tube.

The Single Tube Camera: Specification performance of single tube color cameras is dependent on each camera's deflection scanning. Creation of the red, blue and green colors is taken from the frequency of the horizontal scan and consistently maintained field to field by the vertical scan. For this reason, the criteria for adjusting deflection is recovery of the color signal, (as opposed to minimizing geometric distortion in the three tube color camera). This specification is not listed for single tube color cameras.

In the single tube color camera sensitivity is reduced by the absence of two additional tubes. In addition, incoming light to the single tube is further reduced as the light must pass through the dichroic filter. For this specification, the camera is rated at the widest lens opening with the gain boost on. Unlike the three tube camera, whose specification rating permits operating at lower light conditions, the single tube camera has no margin below its sensitivity specification. Operation with the gain boosted results in the lowest signal-to-noise ratio. Signal-to-noise figures between three tube and single tube cameras can differ by as much as 12 db.

Geometric distortion, reduction in sensitivity and picture resolution are less in single tube cameras than in three tube cameras. Consumer and low-end single tube cameras usually yield horizontal resolution of 250 to 270 lines. High-end and broadcast quality single tube cameras with ''high band'' tubes have resolution specifications of approximately 360 lines.

Glossary

AM Modulation: See Modulated Carrier.

Analog: A continuously varying electronic signal.

Analog Recording: Form of magnetic recording in which the recorded waveform signal maintains the shape of the original signal.

Back Porch: Portion of a composite video signal between the trailing edge of the horizontal sync pulse and the leading edge of the video portion of the signal.

Bandwidth Reduction: See Modulated Carrier.

Baseband Signal: The original video signal, whether analog or digital, that is used to modulate a carrier.

Bias Signal: In magnetic recording systems such as VTRs, the magnetization properties of the videotape do not have a linear characteristic. As the current passing through the recording head's coil increases, the tape's magnetization also increases, however, not in direct proportion. There is a range in which the tape's response is merely linear, meaning that a direct proportion exists between the head coil current and the magnetization of the tape. Applying a very high frequency sine wave to the head coil keeps the overall recording operation within the linear portion of the tape's magnetization characteristic. In video recording, the stationary audio heads, those which record the linear audio tracks, must receive a bias signal to provide a faithful audio recording.

Black Burst: See Color Reference Burst.

Breezeway: Portion of the video signal's back porch between the training edge of horizontal sync and the start of color reference burst.

Capstan: Rotating shaft on a videotape recorder transport path. The capstan controls the tape speed as it travels from the supply reel to the take-up reel.

Cathode Ray Tube (CRT): TV picture tube.

Chrominance: Chrominance typically stands for the color component of the television signal. Chrominance has two components—hue and saturation. Hue is defined as tint. It is the characteristic of the color itself. Saturation indicates the degree to which the color is diluted by luminance, or white light.

Color Bars: Standard color test signal, displayed as rows ("bars") of color.

Color Reference Burst: A signal inserted on the back porch of horizontal sync. When compared to the color subcarrier signal, the color reference burst determines the hue of a video image.

Color Subcarrier: Carrier frequency (3.58 MHz) on which the color signal information is impressed.

Component: Components are the sync, luminance and chrominance elements of a television signal. In terms of videotape formats, the term component refers to the methods used by recorders to process the visible (viewable) video signal. In component processing the viewable video signal is divided into three parts: one luminance and two chrominance. The component elements of the video signal are Y (luminance), I and Q (color components), or Y (luminance) and R-Y, B-Y (color components).

Composite Video: The video signal is composed of a number of elements that make up the television picture. Sync provides picture stability, luminance provides picture brightness and chrominance provides color. When referring to television, composite video means that the video signal contains sync as well as picture information. When composite is used in terms of videotape format, it means that the video signal is provided only in a composite form as both an input and output.

Control Pulse: When a video recorder is making a recording, it not only puts video and audio on the tape, but also a synchronizing signal called the control pulse, which will be used for playback. The control pulse is placed on its own track, called the control track. During playback, the control pulse is used by the servo circuits to maintain tracking.

Decibels (db): A decibel is a unit of measure used to compare the same parameter of two different signals. Such parameters might be voltage or power levels. In common usage, when comparing the voltage level of a signal to the voltage level of any unwanted noise, for example, we will find that the desired signal might be thousands of times higher than the noise. In order to reduce the seemingly large values derived from such comparisons, the unit of the Bel (named for Alexander G.Bell) was established. The further reduction of this number by one tenth (deci) of a Bel became the common unit of measure. The deciBel (db) is a logarithmic comparison of the two signals.

Digital: Electronic recording system which converts the analog signal into a series of discrete binary bits.

Electronic Field Production (EFP): Videotape production using single camera film-style shooting technique.

Electronic News Gathering (ENG): Using portable video equipment to record news events.

Field: Half of one television field (262.5 horizontal lines at 59.94 Hz, NTSC).

FM Modulation: See Modulated Carrier.

Frequency Response: Frequency response is the measurement used to determine how effectively a piece of video equipment handles a range of frequencies. In electronics equipment the higher the frequency, the more its amplitude is suppressed by video processing circuits. Since picture details are a function of frequency response—the greater the frequency response, the greater the picture details, or resolution. Frequency response is expressed in terms of 3 db down from the frequency that is reproduced at the highest amplitude.

Front Porch: Portion of the composite video signal that starts at the trailing edge of the picture information and ends at the leading edge of the horizontal sync.

Gain: Amplitude or strength of a signal.

Generation Loss: Generation loss is the accumulative degradation of a video signal recorded on tape. When a video signal from a camera is recorded on tape, it is called the first generation recording. A copy of this tape would be a second generation recording, and so on. It is not unusual for production people to create effects in progressive stages, thereby exceeding 15 or more generations. The better the recorder, the higher its multi-generation capability.

Gray Scale: Range of luminance levels from black to white.

Guard Band: Blank section of tape used to prevent crosstalk interference between audio record tracks.

Head: Magnetic device in a videotape recorder used to record, erase or reproduce video or audio signals.

Hertz: A unit of frequency equal to one cycle per second. Kilohertz (kHz)—1000 cycles per second. Megahertz (MHz)—1,000,000 cycles per second.

Horizontal Blanking Interval: Portion of the composite video signal between the end of picture information on one line and the start of picture information on the next line.

Horizontal Sync: The portion of the composite video signal that synchronizes the scanning electron beam of the TV monitor so that each line of picture information will start at the same lateral position during scanning.

I Signal: The I signal represents color such as orange or cyan. The human eye sees detail best in this range of hues. In the Y, I and Q color transmission system the I signal has a 1.5 MHz bandwidth (compared with 0.5 MHz for other color signals)—this accounts for its ability to reproduce details.

Interlaced Scanning: NTSC television scanning process in which two fields of video are interlaced to create one full frame of video.

IRE: Institute of Radio Engineers.

Jitter: Jumping or instability in the TV picture, often caused by synchronization or tracking errors.

Linear Tape Speed: Linear tape speed should not be confused with linear (or non-linear) systems. Linear tape speed is the name given to the parameter of the speed of the tape in its path. In video, the speed of the tape as it moves through its path varies greatly between formats. There are three speeds in consumer VHS. These are SP, LP and SLP.

Longitudinal Time Code: Type of SMPTE time code that is recorded on the audio track of a videotape.

Luminance: Luminance is the black and white component of the television signal. The amount of luminance contained in a video signal is directly related to the amount of light intensity. The human eye views this as brightness. Luminance also plays a part in color signals. In the absence of luminance, color signals are black.

Modulated Carrier: This term is used primarily to designate a type of modulation system. A modulation system changes a simple sine wave. In amplitude modulation (AM), the modulating signal (a video or audio signal) changes the amplitude of a high-frequency sine wave. The recording system, then, only has to record this one particular frequency. In frequency modulation systems (FM), the modulating audio or video signal changes the instantaneous frequency of the sine wave. FM, in many cases, is the preferred method since it is immune to any amplitude non-linearities of the recording system. In an FM video recording system, the video input analog or digital signal is used to frequency modulate the high-frequency sine wave. This modulation action produces a band of frequencies centered around the carrier frequency (the original sine wave). There is not, however, a tremendous shift from the carrier frequency, certainly not as large as the range encountered in the original video signal. Video signals range typically from 30 Hz to 4.5 MHz (a span of 14 octaves). When a video signal is used to FM modulate a high-frequency sine wave, the result is a band of frequencies spanning just a few octaves. This reduction in the range of octaves is called bandwidth reduction.

Noise: Elements that interfere with the clarity and purity of the TV image.

Non-Linear Characteristics: Non-linear characteristics describe how a recording system responds to an applied input signal. A system that produces an exactly proportional output or response to a varying input is said to be operating in a linear fashion. The term is borrowed from mathematicians' jargon in which a comparison is made between the input and output of a system, in graph form. The proportional relationship does not have to be one-to-one, it can be exactly double, triple, half or quarter (or anything else) of the input at any particular time, voltage or frequency. Systems in which the proportionality changes with respect to time, frequency and amplitude are non-linear systems.

NTSC Color Video Standard: The U.S. standard for color TV transmission, called for 525 lines of information, scanned at a rate of 30 frames per second.

Peak White: Brightest level of the video signal.

Pedestal: Reference black level of the video signal (7.5 units for color, 10 units for black and white). Also called setup.

Piezo-electric Crystal: A piezo-electric crystal is a salt crystal capable of delivering an electrical signal output when it is twisted or flexed. The earliest applications of these crystals were in crystal phonograph cartridges. Today, video heads can be mounted on piezoelectric crystals. These are then mounted into head cylinders. If a voltage is applied to the crystal, it will flex, thereby changing the physical position of the video head. This allows the head to properly trace the video tracks when the videotape is played back.

Pinch Roller: A rubber roller on the tape transport path that presses the videotape against the capstan.

Q Signal: In Y, I and Q transmission systems the I and Q components create the complete color signal. The hues contained in the Q signal are darker than those in the I component and represent purples and greens. Due to its hues, both the human eye and the television system de-emphasize details. The resulting bandwidth is 0.5 MHz or one third that of the I signal.

Raster: Area of the TV picture tube that is scanned by the electron beam.

Recorded Wavelength: The recorded wavelength is the space required on the tape to record a particular frequency. When a high-frequency video signal is to be played back from a tape, the gap length of the playback head must be small enough to accommodate it. That is, video head gaps that are very small have better high-frequency response. Of equal importance is the writing speed—the equivalent video head-to-tape speed. If the writing speed is kept high, then the recorded wavelength for high video frequencies can be kept longer—thereby making the manufacture of video heads easier (since the gap length need not be extremely small).

Resolution: Amount and degree of detail in the video image, measured along both the horizontal and vertical axes.

RGB: Red, green and blue, the primary colors in color video.

Segmented Format: A segmented format requires multiple head passes to record a single video field. An individual video head used in a segmented format will only record a portion of the video field. Segmented formats require multiple head switching systems in playback to reconstruct the complete video field.

Signal-to-Noise Ratio: The signal-to-noise ratio is a logarithmic comparison of a video signal (or audio signal) to the noise found in the recording system. (See Decibel.) When discussing video signals, the signal-to-noise ratio (S/N) of a broadcast recorder is typically 50 dB or greater. Consumer video recorders typically have a video S/N of 42 dB or less. The greater this number, the better the performance.

Sync: Synchronization—usually refers to the pulses necessary to coordinate the operation of several interconnected video components.

Skew: Irregularity in the TV picture caused by improper tape tension or by a difference in head tip penetration during recording and playback on certain VTRs. Skew usually appears as a saw-tooth effect at the edge of the image.

Tape Path: In a tape recorder, the route that the tape travels from the supply reel to the take-up reel is the tape path. In the record mode, recorded signals are placed on the tape as it travels along the tape path. In the playback mode all signals are recovered from the tape. As the tape travels along its path it contacts every head responsible for writing and reading signals.

Target: Photosensitive front surface of a video camera's pickup tube.

Time Compression: Time compression describes the system used to compress the color components of the video signal so they can be recorded on tape. The R-Y and B-Y signals are similar in terms of duration. By compressing them into one duration (one half of their normal period), both signals can be recorded on one video track by one video head. This method of recording allows a great deal of information to be recorded in a small space. During playback the process is reversed to reconstruct the complete video signal.

Writing Speed: Writing speed in video recorders is determined by how fast the video heads move across the tape, in addition to the tape speed.

Y, I and Q Signals: The Y, I and Q signal system was developed to achieve the maximum amount of detail in the transmission of color television signals. In Y, I and Q systems the I and Q signals are 90° out of phase with each other. The difference allows them to be multiplexed and recorded by a signal head in a helical tape wrap system. Y is the luminance component of the video signal. It is the component of the video signal that contains brightness and picture detail.

Y, R-Y, B-Y: As in the Y, I and Q systems, Y, R-Y, B-Y began its existence as a color processing system for television. It is now used to refer to a method of component recording. R-Y and B-Y stand for each of the color signals minus the luminance component. As in the Y, I and Q component system each of the components represents a grouping of colors. In this system each of the color components has a bandwidth of 0.5 MHz.

Index

About The Author

Neil Heller is currently the editor of *Video Manager* magazine, published by Knowledge Industry Publications, Inc. and business manager of Montage Publishing, Inc. Formerly, he served as president and founder of National Servitech, a company that provides technical services and parts to the video security industry. Prior to that, he was director of technical services and product development manager for GYYR Odetics, where he was responsible for writing and conducting technical training programs and service information on microprocessor controlled videotape recorders, both industrial and broadcast. Mr. Heller was producer/director for local public broadcast in New York and California, and for PBS. He has also conducted courses in television production. Other titles Mr. Heller has authored include—*The Great Tape Debates: Evolution of New Video Formats*, published by Knowledge Industry Publications, Inc. and *The Compact Disc Handbook,* published by Howard W. Sams & Company. Mr. Heller has written over 700 articles on new technology and new technology development that have appeared in various publications.